Microsoft Press®
Guide to

DOUBLESPACE™

Microsoft Press®
Guide to
DOUBLESPACE™

Understanding Data

Compression with MS-DOS

6.0 and 6.2

DOUG LOWE

PUBLISHED BY
Microsoft Press
A Division of Microsoft Corporation
One Microsoft Way
Redmond, Washington 98052-6399

Library of Congress Cataloging-in-Publication Data
Lowe, Doug.
    Microsoft press guide to DoubleSpace : understanding data
compression with MS-DOS(R) 6.0 and 6.2 / Doug Lowe.
        p.   cm.
    Includes index.
    ISBN 1-55615-625-1
    1. Data compression (Electronic computers)   2. MS-DOS (Computer
file)   3. DoubleSpace.   I. Title.
QA76.9.D33L68 1993
005.74'6--dc20   93-37545
                                                          CIP

Printed and bound in the United States of America.

1 2 3 4 5 6 7 8 9 AG-M 9 8 7 6 5 4

Distributed to the book trade in Canada by Macmillan of Canada, a division of Canada
Publishing Corporation.

Distributed to the book trade outside the United States and Canada by
Penguin Books Ltd.

Penguin Books Ltd., Harmondsworth, Middlesex, England
Penguin Books Australia Ltd., Ringwood, Victoria, Australia
Penguin Books N.Z. Ltd., 182-190 Wairau Road, Auckland 10, New Zealand

British Cataloging-in-Publication Data available.

DoubleTools and SuperStor are registered trademarks of Addstor, Inc. LANtastic is a
registered trademark of Artisoft, Inc. PC Tools is a trademark of Central Point Software, Inc.
Microsoft, Microsoft Press, MS, and MS-DOS are registered trademarks and DoubleSpace
and Windows are trademarks of Microsoft Corporation. 386MAX is a registered trademark of
Qualitas, Inc. QEMM is a trademark of Quarterdeck Office Systems. Stacker is a registered
trademark of STAC Electronics. The Norton Utilities is a registered trademark of Symantec
Corporation. SyQuest Technology is a registered trademark of SyQuest Technology, Inc.

Acquisitions Editor: Michael Halvorson
Project Editor: Erin O'Connor
Technical Editor: Jim Fuchs

Contents

Acknowledgments

A ton of people helped me with this book.

I'll start with the good folks at Microsoft Press. I thank Mike Halvorson for taking on this project, for getting the 6.2 beta to me so fast, and for humoring my goofy ideas for the cover. Special thanks to project editor Erin O'Connor for keeping this whole project on track, for undangling my participles, and for quoting Housman to me when I needed it most ("Terence, this is stupid stuff"). Thanks also to technical editors Jeff Carey and Jim Fuchs and to all the others at Microsoft Press who did things I don't even know about.

DoubleThanks to William Keener of Microsoft Product Support Services for adding his unique perspective to the manuscript and to David Schott for explaining the mysteries of troubleshooting DoubleSpace in MS-DOS 6.0. And to Ben Slivka, the DoubleGod himself, thanks for reviewing the manuscript, for telling me how Dblspace /defrag *really* works, and for creating a great product.

Thanks also to Corey Tucker and Chuck Runquist of Vertisoft, Inc.; Cris Kukshtel of Addstor, Inc.; and Sioux Flemming, Gary Thomassen, and Jim Sesma of Central Point Software. And of course, mucho thanks to Debbie, Rebecca, Sarah, and Bethany, who put up with a lot while I wrote this little book.

Introduction

DoubleSpace is the data compression feature of MS-DOS 6.0 and 6.2. It doubles the capacity of your hard disk by squeezing your data so that it can be stored on disk more efficiently. Once you've installed DoubleSpace, this compression is entirely automatic. You won't even know it's there.

Well, that's the party line, anyway. The reality is that DoubleSpace imposes a new level of complexity on you and the way you use your computer. To make the best use of DoubleSpace, you have to understand what it is and how it works. You also have to know how it affects the way you use other MS-DOS commands, and you have to know how to use its central control command, Dblspace.

IS THIS BOOK FOR YOU?

Microsoft has estimated that more than 60 percent of the computer users who installed MS-DOS 6.0 also used DoubleSpace. That puts the number of DoubleSpace users at more than 4 million even before MS-DOS 6.2 users are taken into account, and like the national debt and the number of hamburgers that have been served at McDonald's, the number of DoubleSpace users is increasing every day.

Regardless of whether you're thinking about joining the ranks of DoubleSpace users, you're a DoubleSpace skeptic, or you're already a convert, I wrote this book with you in mind.

- If you've just installed MS-DOS 6.0 or 6.2 but haven't installed DoubleSpace because you're not sure what it is, how it works, or whether it's safe, this book is just what you need. It will clear up all your confusion about DoubleSpace so that you'll be able to install it and use it with confidence.

- If you haven't bought or upgraded to MS-DOS 6.0 or 6.2 because you're skeptical about the DoubleSpace incentive, you should definitely read this book. It will give you a chance to learn all about DoubleSpace so that you can make your decision based on facts rather than rumors.

- If you've already installed MS-DOS 6.0 or 6.2 and DoubleSpace, all the better. This book will show you the ins and outs of using DoubleSpace in ways you probably haven't thought of. You'll go beyond a basic understanding of DoubleSpace to complete mastery of it.

VERSION MANIA: MS-DOS 6.0 AND 6.2

Microsoft introduced MS-DOS 6.0 in March 1993. MS-DOS 6.0 improved upon MS-DOS 5.0 by adding a suite of much-needed utility programs: a sophisticated backup program (Msbackup), an antivirus program (Msav), a disk defragmenter (Defrag), a memory optimizer (Memmaker), a diagnostic program (MSD), and two utilities designed specifically for laptop users (Interlnk and Power). But the cornerstone of MS-DOS 6.0 was its disk compression program, DoubleSpace.

Considering all of the new features included with MS-DOS 6.0, you'd think that the Microsoft MS-DOS developers would have asked for some time off. But as soon as MS-DOS 6.0 was finished, they began work on improving both MS-DOS 6.0 and DoubleSpace. In October 1993, Microsoft released MS-DOS 6.2, which includes the following improvements to DoubleSpace:

- ScanDisk, a sophisticated disk analysis and repair tool that checks the internal structure of disk data—regardless of whether the data has been compressed by DoubleSpace—much more thoroughly than the war-weary Chkdsk command. In addition, ScanDisk checks your disk's recording surface for defects, a function that used to require a third-party utility such as *PC Tools* or *The Norton Utilities*. ScanDisk is designed to be used in place of the Chkdsk command. (Chkdsk is still included with MS-DOS 6.2, though—you'll want to use it for quick checks for free space on a disk.)

ScanDisk addresses the most common DoubleSpace safety issue: it ensures that you won't install DoubleSpace on a drive that has unmarked bad clusters.

- Automount, a DoubleSpace feature that makes using compressed floppy disks easier. With the Automount feature enabled, floppy disks and removable drives will be mounted automatically.

- DoubleGuard, a safety feature that helps protect DoubleSpace from the unlikely possibility of corruption by miscreant memory resident programs.

- Uncompress, a feature that lets you easily uncompress your compressed data and remove DoubleSpace. Before MS-DOS 6.2, removing DoubleSpace was a tedious and error-prone manual process.

- The ability to boot clean, without activating DoubleSpace.

- The reduction of DoubleSpace's memory requirement by about 11KB.

MS-DOS 6.2 also includes several improvements unrelated to DoubleSpace:

- A safer implementation of write-caching in SmartDrive, plus the ability to cache CD-ROM drives.

- A single-pass Diskcopy command so that you don't have to swap floppy disks a gazillion times.

- Selective execution of AUTOEXEC.BAT commands when you press F8 at startup. A benefit of this feature is the ability to run any batch file in single-step mode.

- The Dir, Mem, Chkdsk, and Format commands' use of commas when they display big numbers. Now you can tell that 43233443 is 43 million, not 432 thousand, without squinting at the screen.

- The Copy, Xcopy, and Move commands' request for confirmation before they overwrite files.

This book works whether you're using MS-DOS 6.0 or 6.2. Aside from its improvements, the DoubleSpace program hasn't changed fundamentally. In fact, most DoubleSpace operations are identical in MS-DOS 6.0 and

6.2. Wherever there's a variation between MS-DOS 6.0 and 6.2, I'll be sure to make the difference crystal clear.

HOW TO USE THIS BOOK

Like anything new, DoubleSpace can seem confusing at first. But it isn't rocket science. No Ph.D. is required. Just a little attentiveness, some patience, and a basic familiarity with MS-DOS.

- Chapter 1 is a gentle introduction to DoubleSpace that deals with that nagging question *Is it safe?*

- Chapter 2 describes how DoubleSpace works in lay terms. Its main purpose is to convince you that DoubleSpace isn't witchcraft.

- Chapter 3 shows you how to safely install DoubleSpace. It describes what you should do before and after you install DoubleSpace so that you can avoid the most common DoubleSpace pitfalls.

- Chapter 4 explores how DoubleSpace changes the way you work with your computer—how you back up compressed data, how to find out a file's compression ratio, and so on. More specifically, this chapter looks at the other MS-DOS commands in relation to DoubleSpace.

- Chapter 5 introduces you to the ubiquitous Dblspace program, the control center from which you manage DoubleSpace operations.

- Chapter 6 helps you set up more than one compressed drive and explains how DoubleSpace assigns drive letters to compressed drives and regular hard drives.

- Chapter 7 shows you what you need to know to use compressed floppy drives and compressed removable hard drives. It talks about MS-DOS 6.2's Automount feature too.

- Chapter 8 describes the most common DoubleSpace problems and how to solve them.

- Chapter 9 discusses the relationship between DoubleSpace and *Microsoft Windows*.

- Chapter 10 tells you how to remove DoubleSpace, using the Uncompress feature under MS-DOS 6.2 or manually under MS-DOS 6.0.

- Chapter 11 explains how to convert a compressed drive to DoubleSpace from any other disk compression program.

- Chapter 12 describes several third-party utility programs that work alongside DoubleSpace.

- Chapter 13 is for the technically stout: it takes you inside DoubleSpace so that you'll understand its inner workings. Pocket protectors are required while reading this chapter.

- The appendix is a command summary for quick reference.

If you have MS-DOS 6.0 or 6.2 but have not yet installed DoubleSpace, I suggest that you read at least Chapters 1 through 3 before you compress your disk. You might even want to read the whole book first.

Happy compressing!

You shall have a double portion.

—Isaiah 61:7

Chapter 1

What Is DoubleSpace?

DoubleSpace is a new feature of MS-DOS 6.0 and 6.2 that increases the capacity of your computer's disk drives. It does that by using a special data compression technique to squeeze the data stored on the disk. DoubleSpace is an optional part of MS-DOS 6.0 and 6.2 that's not automatically installed when you run the MS-DOS Setup program. To install DoubleSpace, you must use the Dblspace command at the MS-DOS prompt after you've installed MS-DOS 6.0 or 6.2.

Once installed, DoubleSpace works "on the fly." In other words, it automatically compresses and decompresses data whenever you access your hard disk. This compression and decompression occurs behind the scenes, so you and your programs will be unaware of its operation. The only visible sign that DoubleSpace is working will be the magical transformation of your 80MB disk drive into a 160MB disk drive.

This chapter is an introduction to DoubleSpace. It answers the most common questions about DoubleSpace: *What exactly does DoubleSpace do? Will it really double my disk? Is it safe?* And so on.

WHAT EXACTLY DOES DOUBLESPACE DO?

How does DoubleSpace pull off the seemingly impossible task of transforming your uncomfortably small 80MB disk into an enormous 160MB disk with more free space than you know what to do with? Is it magic, wizardry, witchcraft? None of the above.

Here's a hint. DoubleSpace doesn't really make your disk any bigger than it was before. It doesn't somehow find space between the sectors of your disk drive or cause the read/write heads to write smaller bits.

1

Instead, DoubleSpace does what we wish politicians would do: it eliminates waste so that less disk space is required to store your files. DoubleSpace doesn't really transform an 80MB disk drive into a 160MB disk drive. It compresses 160MB of disk files to half their original size, so that only 80MB of disk space is required to store them.

DoubleSpace attacks the waste problem with a one-two punch. First, it uses disk space more efficiently by allocating disk space to your files one *sector* at a time rather than in groups of sectors called *clusters*. Second, it compresses the disk data by ferreting out duplicated information. Most of the files on your computer have a surprising amount of redundant information in them. Think, for example, about how many times the word *DoubleSpace* appears in this chapter.

I'll go into DoubleSpace's methods of allocating space for your files and compressing data in more detail in the next chapter. If these ideas don't make a lot of sense to you right now, don't worry. They'll make perfect sense to you after you read the next chapter.

CAN IT REALLY DOUBLE MY DISK?

DoubleSpace reports compression results in terms of ratios. The higher the ratio, the more DoubleSpace was able to compress a file. If DoubleSpace says that a file's compression ratio is 2 to 1, it has squeezed the file into half the space the file required uncompressed. A compression ratio of 3 to 1 means that DoubleSpace has squeezed the file to one-third its original size.

Some kinds of files compress better than others. Here are some typical compression ratios for various types of files:

Executable programs (.EXE)	1.4 to 1
Microsoft Word documents (.DOC)	2.8 to 1
Microsoft Excel documents (.XLS)	3.3 to 1
Bitmaps (.BMP)	4.0 to 1
ASCII text files (.TXT, .BAT)	2.0 to 1
Sound files (.WAV)	1.1 to 1
Compressed files (.ZIP)	1.0 to 1

For most users, the compression ratios for all of the files on a compressed disk will average out to about 2 to 1. That's why Microsoft claims that DoubleSpace effectively doubles the capacity of your hard disk. Keep in mind, though, that Microsoft's claim that it doubles your disk capacity is a bit like an auto manufacturer's claims for a car's gas mileage. Your results will vary, depending on the mix of the various types of files on your hard disk.

It's interesting to note which kinds of files compress poorly or not at all. Did you notice in the list of typical compression ratios that the sound files (.WAV) compressed at only 1.1 to 1? That's because sound files contain data that seems random to DoubleSpace. Since there's not much repetition in random data, DoubleSpace isn't able to compress these files. And files that have already been compressed by a compression program such as *PKZIP* can't be compressed further by DoubleSpace. That's why the ratio for .ZIP files is 1.0 to 1.

IS IT SAFE?

Shortly after MS-DOS 6.0 was released, some users complained that DoubleSpace was unreliable, that it "trashed my data" or "totaled my disk." A major magazine reported that of the machines on which it tested DoubleSpace use, 50 percent ran into severe problems. Some users even accused Microsoft of releasing DoubleSpace without adequate testing.

Is DoubleSpace safe?

Rest assured that it is. DoubleSpace is not bug-ridden, inherently unstable, or poorly tested. In fact, it is one of the most thoroughly tested computer programs ever released.

DoubleSpace makes use of data compression techniques developed in the 1970s and in wide use in backup programs, tape drive storage, stand-alone compression programs such as *PKZIP,* and competing data compression programs such as *Stacker* and *DoubleDisk.*

With the introduction of MS-DOS 6.2, Microsoft made DoubleSpace even safer. They improved the DoubleSpace installation procedure so that it now analyzes the surface of your disk drive to make sure that the drive is reliable. And they've added a new feature called *DoubleGuard,* which helps detect software conflicts.

With or without the safety improvements provided with MS-DOS 6.2, the problem with DoubleSpace has not been that it's unsafe but that it's complicated. Most of the problems users have experienced with DoubleSpace have been caused by, well, let's be gentle, misunderstanding on the user's

What's Different for MS-DOS 6.2?

DoubleSpace is essentially the same whether you're using MS-DOS 6.0 or 6.2. However, Microsoft has improved DoubleSpace for MS-DOS 6.2 in several ways:

- The DoubleSpace installation routine now invokes the new MS-DOS 6.2 ScanDisk command to analyze the surface of your disk drive. This locks out any surface defects that might otherwise cause problems.

- DoubleSpace can now automatically access compressed floppy drives and removable disks even while *Windows* is running.

- DoubleSpace now requires less conventional or upper memory: 37KB instead of 43KB (33KB without Automount).

- DoubleSpace now includes a safety feature, called *Double-Guard,* that constantly monitors its memory buffers, warning of any corruption introduced by incompatible software.

- The Dblspace command now includes several switches that let you change settings in the DBLSPACE.INI control file so that you no longer have to edit the file directly.

- You can boot clean, without activating DoubleSpace, by pressing Ctrl+F5 or Ctrl+F8 when you see the message *Starting MS-DOS.*

Even if you've already upgraded to MS-DOS 6.0 and installed DoubleSpace, these improvements are well worth the small cost of upgrading to 6.2.

part. Too many users have installed DoubleSpace after reading nothing about it other than what's printed on the outside of the MS-DOS 6.0 or 6.2 upgrade box. There's more to using DoubleSpace than typing *dblspace* at the command prompt.

This book is loaded with DoubleSpace safety tips. Chapter 3 will show you how to install DoubleSpace safely. Chapter 4 will show you how to use DoubleSpace safely with a variety of MS-DOS commands. And Chapter 8 will show you how to solve DoubleSpace problems if they arise.

WILL IT SLOW DOWN MY COMPUTER?

If you have an aging 286 system, you probably don't have enough computing horsepower to run DoubleSpace without noticing some slowdown in processing speed.

If you have a modern 386 or 486 computer, you probably won't notice any slowdown. In fact, your computer might do some operations faster. That's because one of the slowest operations your computer performs is accessing data on the disk. When you use DoubleSpace, your computer does that less often. On today's fastest computers, DoubleSpace can read and decompress compressed data faster than it could read an equivalent amount of uncompressed data.

WHAT ABOUT FLOPPIES AND REMOVABLE DISKS?

DoubleSpace works with floppy disks as well as with hard disks. If you have a 1.44MB floppy drive, you can compress your disks so that they hold 2.88MB of data. With the cost of disks these days, that can save you a bundle if you use floppies much.

DoubleSpace also works with removable hard disk drives such as those made by Bernoulli and SyQuest. Here, too, the increase in disk capacity is welcome, considering the cost of cartridges for these drives.

The version of DoubleSpace that shipped with MS-DOS 6.0 wasn't quite as elegant as it could have been when it came to supporting floppy disks and removable drives. MS-DOS 6.0 forced you to issue an MS-DOS command before DoubleSpace could access data on a compressed floppy disk. This made it impractical to use compressed floppy disks with *Microsoft Windows.*

Fortunately, MS-DOS 6.2 rectifies this problem by introducing a feature called *Automount,* which eliminates the need to issue an MS-DOS command before accessing either a compressed floppy or a removable compressed drive. With MS-DOS 6.2, compressed floppy disks can be conveniently accessed during a *Windows* session.

Chapter 7 covers the ins and outs of using DoubleSpace with removable disks, including floppies.

WHAT ABOUT *MICROSOFT WINDOWS?*

DoubleSpace is a godsend for *Microsoft Windows* users. One basic fact of life for *Windows* users is that you *never* have enough disk space. It's not uncommon for an application program for *Windows* to come on 10 disks and require 20MB or more of disk space. Graphics files and sound files take up an inordinate amount of disk space. Ever since I switched to *Windows,* it's been a constant struggle to keep free space on my disk.

DoubleSpace to the rescue! With DoubleSpace, you'll instantly free up loads of space for those disk-hungry applications for *Windows.*

Of course, you'll eventually fill up your newly doubled disk. If 100MB isn't enough disk space, 200MB isn't either. DoubleSpace doesn't prevent the inevitable, but it does put it off long enough to give you and your disk some much-needed breathing room.

WHAT'S THE BAD NEWS?

DoubleSpace isn't without its disadvantages. There's no such thing as a free lunch.

Installing DoubleSpace is pretty much a one-way street. It's difficult to remove DoubleSpace once you've installed it, although it can be done. True, MS-DOS 6.2 comes with a DoubleSpace uninstaller that makes it easier to remove DoubleSpace. But if you've added more files to your hard drive than would fit before you compressed your disk, the only way to remove DoubleSpace is to get rid of some of your files first. (If you do decide to remove DoubleSpace, you'll find instructions for doing that in Chapter 10.)

DoubleSpace requires additional memory. With MS-DOS 6.0, DoubleSpace requires 43KB. With MS-DOS 6.2, Microsoft has managed to reduce the memory requirement to 33KB (37KB if Automount is used). If you have a 386 or better processor and you don't use a memory manager such as QEMM-386 or 386MAX, the improved memory management features of MS-DOS 6.0 and 6.2 should more than make up for DoubleSpace's additional memory requirement. If you do use a memory manager, you might not be able to spare the extra memory. Chapter 3 shows you how to make sure you can afford the memory before you try to install DoubleSpace.

In addition, the mere presence of DoubleSpace on your system complicates your computing life. DoubleSpace is as unobtrusive as can be, but it still manages to introduce all sorts of considerations, some subtle, some dramatic. These considerations are discussed in detail in Chapter 4, "Working with Compressed Data."

SUMMARY

DoubleSpace is a boon if you're tight on disk space.

- DoubleSpace works in two ways: it improves on the MS-DOS scheme for allocating disk space to your files, and it squeezes repetitive data out of your files so that they require less disk space.

- The compression ratio DoubleSpace achieves for various files depends on the kinds of files they are. Overall, though, DoubleSpace achieves close to a 2 to 1 compression ratio.

- DoubleSpace has been thoroughly tested. Although it's not a simple program, it is safe enough if you take appropriate precautions when you install and use it. The new ScanDisk command in MS-DOS 6.2 makes installing and using DoubleSpace even safer.

- DoubleSpace may slow down your computer if you have an older 286 processor. If you have a modern 386 or 486 processor, you probably won't notice any performance slowdown as a result of using

DoubleSpace. In fact, you might actually notice that performance improves.

■ DoubleSpace can be used with hard disks, floppy disks, and removable hard disks.

■ DoubleSpace is especially useful for *Windows* users, who are always running out of disk space.

■ DoubleSpace is difficult to remove if your compressed disk would be too full uncompressed. You'll have to remove some files first.

■ With MS-DOS 6.0, DoubleSpace requires an additional 43KB of memory. The MS-DOS 6.2 version of DoubleSpace requires only 33KB or 37KB depending on whether you use Automount.

I can't come back...I don't know how it works!

—*The Wizard of Oz*

Chapter 2

How DoubleSpace Works

This chapter is an introduction to the inner workings of DoubleSpace. It doesn't present all the details of how DoubleSpace works—I've saved that for the last chapter—but it will tell you just enough to persuade you that DoubleSpace doesn't rely on magic, voodoo, or wizardry to compress your data. Yes, DoubleSpace is a complicated program, but it is after all just a program.

We'll start by looking at how disk drives work. Then, we'll examine the way MS-DOS keeps track of the files on a disk. Finally, we'll consider how DoubleSpace extends the standard MS-DOS file facilities to support compressed data.

HOW A DISK DRIVE WORKS

If you could take apart your computer's hard disk, it would look something like Figure 2-1 on the next page. As you can see, the most obvious feature inside the hard disk is one or more *disk platters*. These platters are coated with a magnetic material similar to the coating on magnetic tape so that information can be recorded on them. The platters are connected to a motor that spins them at a high rate of speed, typically 3500 to 4500 RPM.

At the end of the *arm* that reaches out across each platter is a *read/write head*, a device that can record information on the disk or read information that's stored on the disk. There's one read/write head for each *recording surface* on each platter, and each platter has two recording surfaces

9

Figure 2-1. *Inside a hard disk.*

(top and bottom). So a disk drive that contains three disk platters has six read/write heads.

The arm the read/write heads are mounted on can be moved in and out across the surface of the platter to read or write information at different locations on the platter. The arms move together as an assembly, so the read/write heads are always positioned over the same disk location on each of the platters.

To read data from or write data to a particular location on the disk, the disk drive first moves the read/write head mechanism to the correct track. Then, it selects the read/write head for the surface that contains the desired location. Finally, it waits for the desired track location to approach the head—remember that the platters are spinning beneath the read/write heads. At just the right moment, a magnet in the read/write head is activated to record the data on the track (for a write) or to "listen" to the data previously recorded (for a read).

Binary Magic

The disk platters are where information is stored, but how is the data recorded? How does your computer reduce the numbers in your spreadsheet or the words in your proposal to a form that can be stored on the magnetic platters of a disk drive?

The answer takes me back to my seventh grade math class. My math teacher, Mr. Arnold, thought it would be fun to broaden the horizons of a group of unruly 13-year-olds by showing us that the counting system we use, called the *decimal system,* or *base-10,* is based on the number 10 only because we humans have 10 fingers. He showed us that a counting system can be built just as well around any other number. If dinosaurs had not become extinct, we would probably all know how to multiply and divide in base-6.

To understand other number bases, you have to go even further back than the seventh grade, all the way to the second grade, when you learned about carrying and borrowing to do simple addition and subtraction. Consider a number like 432. Every second grader knows that the 2 represents 2 because it's in the "ones place," the 3 represents 30 because it's in the "tens place," and the 4 represents 400 because it's in the "hundreds place."

What the second grader doesn't know yet is that each of these places corresponds to a power of 10: the ones place is 10 to the power of 0, or 10^0 (any number raised to the power of 0 is 1); the tens place is 10^1 (any number raised to the power of 1 equals itself); the hundreds place is 10^2 (10 times 10, or 100). So the decimal number 432 is $(4 \times 100) + (3 \times 10) + (2 \times 1)$.

Another number base would work the same way, but it would use powers of a number other than 10 to determine the values of its successive digits. For example, in base-7, you don't have the "ones place," the "tens place," and the "hundreds place." Instead, you have the "ones place," the "sevens place," and the "forty-nines place." You just use powers of 7 instead of powers of 10. And you don't use the digits 0 through 9. Instead, you use only the digits 0 through 6.

Mr. Arnold had us counting, adding and subtracting, and even multiplying and dividing in other number bases. He would give us pop quizzes, like What is 43 times 13 in base-7? (622) But his favorite was base-2, also known as the *binary system.* In the binary system, you use only two digits: 0 and 1. In the binary system, a digit is known as a *bit,* which is short for *binary digit.*

In the binary system, each successive digit (right to left) represents a power of 2. For example, consider the binary number 1011. The rightmost digit is multiplied by 2^0 (1). The next digit is multiplied by 2^1 (2). The next digit is multiplied by 2^2 (4). And the leftmost digit is multiplied by 2^3 (8). Thus, the binary number 1011 is $(1 \times 8) + (0 \times 4) + (1 \times 2) + (1 \times 1)$, or decimal 11.

Mr. Arnold told us that the binary system would play a big role in our futures because it was the counting system used by those new-fangled inventions called computers. I didn't pay much attention at the time, but he was right, of course. Computers use the binary system because its two digits—1 and 0—can correspond to two states of electricity—on and off. Thus, computers can easily represent binary values using electronic circuits. And they can electronically record binary values on the platters of a disk.

Bytes, Kilobytes, and Megabytes

A group of 8 bits is called a *byte*. With 8 bits, a byte can be used to store 256 different values. The value of a byte can represent a number, but it's more likely to represent a single character of information.

To represent characters, a code known as *ASCII* is used. ASCII (pronounced ASK-ee) is simply a list of the letters, numerals, and special symbols that are assigned to each of the 256 possible values that a byte can hold. For example, ASCII says that the letter *A* is represented by the number 65 and that an asterisk (*) is represented by the number 42.

You can think of every byte as standing for a character. For example, the word "byte" itself requires 4 bytes to store. The preceding sentence (including the space characters) requires 61 bytes to store. A typical paragraph requires 500 or so bytes. And a page of text requires about 2000 bytes.

To make it easier to refer to large numbers of bytes, the terms *kilobyte* and *megabyte* are often used. A kilobyte (or *KB*) is about 1000 bytes, while a megabyte (or *MB*) is about 1,000,000 bytes. I say *about* here because the terms kilobyte and megabyte both refer to powers of 2, not to decimal values. Strictly speaking, a kilobyte is 1024 (2^{10}) bytes. In practice, it's common to drop the extra 24 and think of a kilobyte as 1000 bytes. Similarly, a megabyte is actually 1,048,576 (2^{20}) bytes. Again, though, it's common to think of a megabyte as an even million bytes.

To put these terms into perspective, note that the size of a typical file is measured in kilobytes. The word processing file that contains this chapter requires about 20KB of disk storage. The capacity of most disk drives is measured in megabytes. The computer I'm using to write this book has a disk drive that can hold 170MB of data. That's enough to hold almost 10,000 chapters the size of this one. Unfortunately, I'm not nearly prolific enough to fill this disk with chapter files anytime soon.

However, it's amazing how quickly even a 170MB disk drive can fill up with files other than chapter files. For example, I recently bought a sound card for my PC. In just two short weeks, I've accumulated nearly 7MB of sound files, some of it indispensable stuff like Chief Inspector Clouseau asking, *Does your dog bite?* or Captain Kirk saying, *Everybody remember where we parked.* If it weren't for DoubleSpace, my 170MB disk wouldn't be nearly big enough for all of my important files!

Tracks and Sectors

Does the computer store data on my 170MB hard drive in a continuous stream of 170 million bytes? Not hardly. To make the large amount of data stored on a disk drive more manageable, a computer uses the time-honored technique known as *divide and conquer.* It divides this large amount of storage space into chunks called *tracks* and *sectors.*

The read/write heads record data on each recording surface in a number of concentric rings called *tracks,* as shown in Figure 2-2.

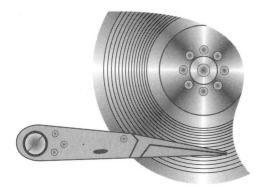

Figure 2-2. *Tracks on a disk surface.*

The number of tracks on each surface depends on the size of the disk drive. My 170MB disk drive has 1009 tracks on each of its six recording surfaces.

Data is written to each track in groups of 512 bytes known as *sectors*. Each track has the same number of sectors. In the case of my typical 170MB drive, each track has 55 sectors. At 512 bytes each, that's more than 25KB per track. Multiply the number of sectors per track (55) times the number of tracks per surface (1009) times the number of surfaces on the disk (6), and you get the total number of sectors on the disk (332,970). Multiply the

Drive Interfaces

Disk drives are not capable of communicating directly with the computer's CPU. A special interface card is required. It's the interface card that manages the details of accessing data on the disk, freeing the computer's main processor for other work. Interface cards and disk drives are not interchangeable; you must make sure they're properly matched.

Over the years, several different types of disk interfaces have emerged. The oldest style, known as ST-506, is found mostly on older XT and AT computers. The ST-506 interface was fine for the original hard disk computers, which were slow and had limited disk capacities of 10 or 20 megabytes. For larger disks and faster processors, an improved interface was needed. For a while, the *ESDI* interface was popular. Today, though, most new computers come with disk drives that use the *IDE* or *SCSI* interface.

With both IDE and SCSI interfaces, most of the interface circuitry is located on the disk itself rather than on a separate interface card. That frees the disk manufacturers to be more innovative in their disk designs. For example, IDE drives can store more sectors on the tracks near the outside of the disk platter because those tracks are longer than the ones near the inside of the platter. That increases the capacity of the drive without adding platters.

DoubleSpace operates the same whether your disk uses an IDE or a SCSI interface, and it even works on older ST-506 and ESDI disks.

total number of sectors by the size of each sector (512 bytes) to get the total capacity of the disk (in this case, 170,480,640 bytes). This number will vary, of course, because, as the sidebar on the preceding page explains, some tracks can store more sectors than others.

Every sector on a disk has a unique sector number. That way, the disk drive can directly access any sector. Each sector's number is recorded in the sector along with the 512 bytes of data and an error correction code that is used to make sure the data has been stored correctly.

HOW MS-DOS KEEPS TRACK OF YOUR FILES

Sector numbers are all the disk drive needs to access any of the sectors on a hard disk, but they're not enough to keep track of the hundreds or thousands of files a typical user keeps on his or her hard disk. To do that, MS-DOS uses a simple record keeping system that maintains a list of the names of all your files and of the sectors that are assigned to each file. This record keeping system is created on the drive when you use the MS-DOS Format command.

Clusters (aka Allocation Units)

You already know that data is recorded on disk in 512-byte sectors. To simplify its record keeping, MS-DOS doesn't track the individual sectors on your disk. Instead, it tracks the sectors in groups called *clusters*. The size of each cluster depends on the disk drive, but most hard disks today use 4, 8, or 16 sectors per cluster. (The People Who Make the Rules recently decided that the term *cluster* should be replaced with the more friendly and inclusive term *allocation unit* from now on. Fat chance.)

Each cluster on a disk has a unique *cluster number*. MS-DOS determines the starting sector number for a given cluster by multiplying the cluster number by the number of sectors (usually 4, 8, or 16) in each cluster.

One inherent disadvantage of using clusters to track sectors is that the smallest file you can create on disk will take up at least the space of one cluster. For example, if your disk uses 8-sector clusters, the smallest file you can create will occupy 4KB of disk space (8 sectors at 512 bytes per sector). That's because MS-DOS can't allocate just part of a cluster.

The Chkdsk Command

Among other things, the MS-DOS Chkdsk command displays information about the capacity of your disk drives. Type the command *chkdsk* without any parameters, and you'll get a report that looks something like this:

```
Volume DRIVE_C      created 02-23-1993 8:08p
Volume Serial Number is 1A57-A047

72,214,528 bytes total disk space
    73,278 bytes in 2 hidden files
    30,720 bytes in 12 directories
60,555,264 bytes in 386 user files
    61,440 bytes in bad sectors
11,493,376 bytes available on disk

     2,048 bytes in each allocation unit
    35,261 total allocation units on disk
     5,612 available allocation units on disk

   655,360 total bytes memory
   619,264 bytes free
```

In this example, you can see that the total capacity of the disk is about 72MB, and that only about 11MB of this space is free. You can also see that the cluster size is 2048, which means that each cluster has 4 sectors. Of the 35,261 total clusters on the disk, 5612 are unused and available for files.

You can also use the Chkdsk command (or in MS-DOS 6.2, the ScanDisk command) to check the integrity of the MS-DOS directory and FAT structures. You'll learn more about that in Chapter 4, "Working with Compressed Data."

The File Allocation Table

To keep track of the clusters, MS-DOS sets up a *File Allocation Table,* or *FAT,* near the beginning of every disk. The FAT entry contains a number for every cluster on the disk. These entries are stored in sequence, so that the first FAT cluster entry corresponds to the first cluster on the disk, the second entry corresponds to the second cluster, and so on.

The contents of each FAT entry indicates whether or not the cluster has been allocated to a file. If a cluster doesn't belong to a file, the cluster's FAT entry contains a 0. If a cluster does belong to a file, its FAT entry contains the number of the next cluster that also belongs to the file. The FAT entry for the last cluster that belongs to a file contains a special code indicating the end of the file. In this way, all of the clusters used by a file are chained together in the FAT.

Consider these FAT entries:

Entry	Value
100	0
101	0
102	103
103	105
104	0
105	106
106	EOF

Here, clusters 100, 101, and 104 are not used by any files, so MS-DOS can use them for new files. The remaining clusters are allocated to a file. If you look at the entry for cluster 102, you'll see that it contains the number 103. That means that the next cluster for the file is cluster 103. If you then look at the entry for cluster 103, you'll see that it chains to cluster 105, which chains to cluster 106. Cluster 106 is the last one for this file, so it contains an End Of File code.

Directories

The one question left unanswered by the File Allocation Table is *Which file does a given cluster belong to?* To answer that question, MS-DOS maintains another table, called the *directory,* on disk. Actually, MS-DOS keeps two types of directories on the disk. Every disk has a *root directory,* which always follows the File Allocation Table on the disk and has a limited size. A *subdirectory* is a special type of file that serves as an extension of the root directory, allowing you to organize your files into logical groupings and allowing you to store more files than the root directory's limited size will allow. A disk can have just one root directory, and the root directory can contain entries for no more than 512 files. However, you can create as many subdirectories as you wish, and there is no limit to the number of file entries in each subdirectory.

A directory (whether the root directory or a subdirectory) contains a simple list of file names along with important information about each file. The most important information kept for each file is the file's starting cluster number. The starting cluster number is the entry that ties the file to the File Allocation Table. To locate a particular file on disk, MS-DOS first reads the file's directory entry to determine the file's first cluster. Then it reads the chain of FAT entries, starting at the file's first cluster, until it reaches an EOF code. Using the first cluster number, MS-DOS can follow the chain to access every cluster that belongs to any file.

PARTITIONS AND LOGICAL DRIVES

We need to look at one more aspect of how MS-DOS deals with disk storage before we jump into DoubleSpace: how MS-DOS divides larger hard disks into partitions and logical drives. Partitions and logical drives (for the moment, we'll regard them as the same thing) are used for a variety of purposes:

- They let you divide a hard disk drive into two or more smaller drives so that you can organize your files more conveniently. For example, you can set up a C drive to hold your program files and a D drive to hold your data files.

- They let you use very large disk drives that MS-DOS can't efficiently support as a single drive. MS-DOS 6.0 can support drives up to 2GB (gigabytes—each gigabyte is 1000 megabytes, or roughly 1 billion bytes), but it would have to use 64-sector clusters to do it (as opposed to the usual 4, 8, or 16 sectors per cluster). At 16 sectors per cluster, the largest drive MS-DOS can support is 512MB. If you have a drive larger than that, you might want to partition it into two drives rather than force the clusters to a larger size. (The cluster size limit exists because the FAT entries limit the total number of usable clusters on a disk to 65,518.)

- Partitions and logical drives were required to support disk drives larger than 32MB under older versions of MS-DOS. This limit was overcome with MS-DOS 4.0, but many systems still have partitions today because they had to be set up that way years ago.

- Originally, partitions were conceived to allow different operating systems to coexist on the same drive. This use of partitions is common today with users of Windows NT or OS/2.

From a practical point of view, we've been thinking of partitions and logical drives as the same thing. There is a technical difference between them, however. The first sector of every disk drive contains a *partition table* that identifies up to four partitions on the drive. Partitions are not optional; every disk must contain at least one. This first partition is called a *primary partition*. When your computer boots, the hard disk's primary partition is assigned drive letter C.

If you want to divide a disk into more than one drive, you must create a second partition, called an *extended partition*. A disk can have only one extended partition. As a result, MS-DOS can use only two of the four possible partitions. The others, if present, must be accessed by other operating systems.

To access the extended partition, you create one or more *logical drives* within it. For example, you might create a single logical drive spanning the entire extended partition. The logical drive in the extended partition would be accessed as drive D. Or you might divide the extended partition into two logical drives, accessed as drives D and E.

Warning: To set up partitions and logical drives, you use the MS-DOS Fdisk command. Fdisk is a loaded weapon, so be careful with it. You can safely use it to display the existing partition structure of your disk, but if you try to make any changes to the partition structure, you might accidentally wipe out the entire disk.

HOW DOUBLESPACE DOUBLES YOUR DISK

OK, that's more than enough background on how MS-DOS stores data on a disk when DoubleSpace isn't involved. How is it that DoubleSpace manages to work within the MS-DOS directory and FAT system to store twice as much data on a disk drive?

In Chapter 1, we looked briefly at DoubleSpace's two-point program for saving disk space: (1) allocating disk space more efficiently and (2) compressing file data.

How DoubleSpace Allocates Disk Space More Efficiently

DoubleSpace uses an improved allocation strategy that eliminates the problem we noted earlier that's inherent in the FAT system: the fact that MS-DOS always allocates whole clusters to a file, even if the particular file doesn't need all of the sectors in a cluster. DoubleSpace allocates sectors to a file one at a time rather than 4, 8, or 16 at a time. If you create a file that requires 13 sectors, DoubleSpace allocates 13 sectors to it, not 16.

One of the keys to understanding DoubleSpace is to realize that it *simulates* a standard FAT disk, where files are allocated disk space in units of whole clusters. A DoubleSpace compressed drive has a File Allocation Table just as a noncompressed drive does. However, the compressed drive avoids the restriction that every cluster must have the same number of sectors and allows clusters to have a variable number of sectors. Each cluster contains just the number of sectors required to store its data in compressed form. So if a cluster's data can be compressed into 3 sectors, only 3 sectors are allocated to that cluster.

You'll learn more about the improved space allocation used by DoubleSpace in Chapter 13, "Inside DoubleSpace."

How DoubleSpace Compresses Data

DoubleSpace's data compression routine seeks out and eliminates the waste that's caused by repetitive data. The computer's ability to process operations at high speeds makes compression methods practical. Consider the following line that might be found in a word processing document:

```
The rain in Spain falls mainly on the plain.
```

Normally, you would expect that the 44 characters (including the space characters) in this line would require 44 bytes of disk space. But this simple line contains a surprising amount of repetition. The letters in and space after the word "in " are repeated in the string of letters and the space at the ends of the words "rain " and "Spain " in the sentence. The sequence "ain" occurs four times, the two-character sequence "n " occurs twice, and the three-character sequence "he " occurs twice. ("T" and "t" have different ASCII codes.)

What if you replaced each duplicate occurrence of one of these strings with a special code, called a *token,* that stood for the duplicated letters? Each token would contain a much shorter number combination that told you how many characters (including spaces) to count backwards in the string and how many characters (including spaces) were duplicated. Then, the line would look like this:

```
The rain <3,3>Sp<9,4>falls m<11,3>ly o<16,2>t<34,3>pl<15,3>.
```

Data compression works because the original form of the string can be reconstructed based on the tokens. For example, when the token <3,3> is encountered, DoubleSpace counts back three characters from the beginning of the token and replaces the token with the three characters it finds there.

The tokens are recorded in the file by means of a special technique that enables them to be stored in less disk space than the bytes they replace. In other words, a token such as <3,3> can be stored in less space than the three bytes it replaces. If the tokens took up more space than the bytes they replaced, there wouldn't be much point in using them.

The key to data compression is the ability to search a string of bytes, iden-tify any duplicated sequences, and replace the repeated bytes with short tokens. With only 44 bytes to work with, a short string like the one above must have a lot of duplication if the data compression is to be worthwhile. But the longer the string, the more likely it is to contain repetitive informa-tion that can be replaced with tokens. DoubleSpace compresses data 8KB at a time, so it can almost always find a significant amount of repetitive information that can be eliminated.

DOUBLESPACE DRIVES

One of the most confusing aspects of using DoubleSpace is the way it affects your drive letters. When you use DoubleSpace to compress a drive, DoubleSpace converts the uncompressed drive into a compressed drive and creates a new drive called the *host drive.*

The Compressed Drive and the CVF

The hardest thing for new DoubleSpace users to understand is the notion of the *Compressed Volume File,* or *CVF.* The CVF is a single file that contains all of the compressed data for a compressed drive. You access the data in the CVF as if the CVF were a separate logical drive with its own drive letter. The drive that holds the CVF is called the *host drive*. Normally, the only reason you need to access the host drive is to store files that can't be compressed, such as the *Windows* permanent swap file.

Figure 2-3 shows a typical 70MB disk drive before and after DoubleSpace has been installed. As you can see, drive C contains 60MB of data and 10MB of free space before DoubleSpace has been installed. After DoubleSpace has been installed, the data from drive C is compressed and stored in the Compressed Volume File. By default, DoubleSpace leaves 2MB of free space on the uncompressed drive. That leaves 68MB for the CVF.

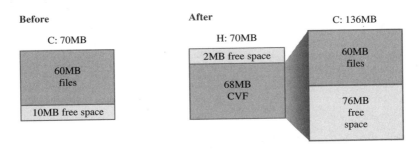

Before

C: 70MB

60MB
files

10MB free space

After

H: 70MB

2MB free space

68MB
CVF

C: 136MB

60MB
files

76MB
free
space

Figure 2-3. *Before and after DoubleSpace.*

To access the compressed data, DoubleSpace treats the CVF as a separate drive, assigning it drive letter C. (In DoubleSpace terminology, we'd say that the CVF is "mounted as drive C.") The compressed drive C contains 60MB of data and a whopping 76MB of free space for a total capacity of 136MB, just under twice the original 70MB capacity of the drive. What about the original drive C, which now contains the CVF? DoubleSpace assigns this host drive another drive letter, in this case H. Although you can access the host drive as drive H, there's usually little reason to. You'll do most of your work with the new compressed drive C. In fact, the compressed drive C will contain the same directories and files as the uncompressed drive C before you installed DoubleSpace. The only difference will be the increased amount of free space.

The Host Drive

A *host drive* is a drive that contains a DoubleSpace Compressed Volume File. Because the CVF is accessed using another drive letter (usually C), there's little reason for you to access the host drive.

If you use the Dir command to display the files on the host drive, you'll discover that although it appears to contain no files, it has little free space. Actually, the host drive contains some very important files you shouldn't tamper with unless you know what you're doing. To protect these files, DoubleSpace gives them the *hidden* attribute so that they don't show up in normal directory listings. You can list them, though, using the MS-DOS Dir /ah command:

1. Log on to the host drive (usually H).

2. Enter the command *dir /ah*. The screen should look something like this one:

```
Volume in drive H is HOST_FOR_C
Volume Serial Number is 1B17-6CD8
Directory of H:\

IO       SYS      40,550 08-11-93   6:20a
MSDOS    SYS      38,138 08-11-93   6:20a
386SPART PAR   8,364,032 08-24-93   9:15a
DBLSPACE 000 231,059,456 08-24-93   9:15a
DBLSPACE BIN      64,246 09-30-93   6:20a
DBLSPACE INI          77 08-24-93   9:15a
        6 file(s)  239,565,475 bytes
                    10,489,856 bytes free
```

The first two files, IO.SYS and MSDOS.SYS, are the two hidden MS-DOS system files that must always be present in the root directory of the boot drive. The fact that they show up here points out that the host drive is actually the boot drive that would normally be accessed as drive C. Because of DoubleSpace, however, the drive letter C is used to access the files in the CVF, and the drive letter H is assigned to the boot drive.

The next file, 386SPART.PAR, is the *Windows* permanent swap file. If you use *Windows,* this file must be on an uncompressed drive. *Windows* hasn't been updated yet to support DoubleSpace compression of this important file. You'll learn how to set up the permanent swap file in Chapter 9, "DoubleSpace and *Microsoft Windows.*"

The next three files are the critical DoubleSpace files. DBLSPACE.000 is the CVF itself. Notice how large it is: at 231MB, it occupies nearly the entire drive. All of the files on the C drive are stored in compressed form within this file, so DoubleSpace wants to take good care of this file. If it were deleted, poof! Your entire C drive would be gone. That's why DoubleSpace gives this file the hidden and read-only attributes. That makes it harder to accidentally delete.

DBLSPACE.BIN is the program that lets MS-DOS access DoubleSpace drives. It must be present in the root directory of the boot drive (drive H).

The last file, DBLSPACE.INI, is an initialization file that contains information about how DoubleSpace is configured. It too must be present in the root directory of the boot drive. I'll explain its innards in Chapter 6, "Using More than One Compressed Drive."

SUMMARY

DoubleSpace effectively doubles the capacity of your hard disk by improving on the way MS-DOS allocates space to files and by compressing file data as it is stored.

- Data is stored on disks in 512-byte sectors.
- MS-DOS allocates space to files in groups of sectors—usually 4, 8, or 16 sectors—called *clusters,* or *allocation units.*
- MS-DOS uses the *File Allocation Table* (the FAT) and directories to keep track of the allocation units associated with each file.
- Large disks can be divided by means of *partitions* and *logical drives.*
- DoubleSpace uses an improved allocation scheme that allocates space one sector at a time, eliminating the waste caused by FAT allocation units.
- DoubleSpace also compresses data by using tokens to eliminate repetitive data from files before they're written to disk.
- All of the data for a compressed drive is stored in a file called the *Compressed Volume File* (the CVF).
- The *host drive* is the drive that contains the CVF. You don't normally need to access it.

Ex-squeeze me?

—*Wayne's World*

Chapter 3

How to Safely Install DoubleSpace

You'll find this message on the back of the MS-DOS 6 User's Guide:

Double your disk easily. Type **dblspace** at the MS-DOS command prompt to double your hard disk space.

Wouldn't it be great if everything in life were so easy? I think the package copywriters got the best of us here. This is like saying,

Marriage is easy! Just say **I do** at the altar prompt.

It's not as easy as it sounds. Just as there's more to marriage than saying, *I do,* there's more to doubling your hard disk space than typing *dblspace* at the command prompt.

This chapter is about installing DoubleSpace. It will walk you through the installation process so that you can see exactly what will happen when you "type **dblspace** at the MS-DOS command prompt." It will tell you what you need to know to answer the questions DoubleSpace Setup will ask you as it works. And, most important, this chapter will show you how to install DoubleSpace *safely*.

In almost all cases, complaints that DoubleSpace was unreliable have turned out to be the result of hasty setup. That's why this chapter starts out by telling you what to do *before* you install DoubleSpace. If you take the precautions I recommend, you'll wonder why anyone complained about how "buggy" DoubleSpace is. You'll be able to grin and say, *Gee, it works just great for me.*

25

WHAT HAPPENS WHEN
YOU INSTALL DOUBLESPACE

Before we go into the precautions you should take before you install DoubleSpace, you might want to know exactly what happens when you install DoubleSpace. Here's what DoubleSpace does when you install it:

- It copies the DoubleSpace system file DBLSPACE.BIN to the root directory of your C drive so that DoubleSpace, once installed, will be activated when you start your computer.

- It sets up a control file named DBLSPACE.INI, also in the root directory of your C drive. This file contains information about your DoubleSpace configuration—which Compressed Volume Files (CVFs) should be mounted as compressed drives and which drive letter to assign to each drive.

- It runs the new ScanDisk command to check the surface of your hard drive for defects (MS-DOS 6.2 only).

- It compresses all of the files on your C drive and stores them in a CVF. You don't install DoubleSpace and then compress your files. Installing DoubleSpace is tantamount to compressing the files on your C drive.

- It runs the Defrag command, new in MS-DOS 6.0, to defragment your disk.

- It mounts the CVF as drive C and assigns another drive letter (typically H) to the uncompressed drive that contains the CVF.

- It adds a command to your CONFIG.SYS file to move the DBLSPACE.BIN file into upper memory (or, if upper memory isn't available, to the bottom of conventional memory).

- It restarts your computer twice as it works.

As you can see, the MS-DOS 6.0 and 6.2 DoubleSpace installation routines are slightly different. With MS-DOS 6.2, DoubleSpace runs the ScanDisk program to verify that your disk is free of undiscovered defects.

WHAT TO DO *BEFORE* YOU INSTALL DOUBLESPACE

The trick to installing DoubleSpace safely is to know what to do *before* you install it. So here's a sequence of preparations and precautions that should make DoubleSpace installation a breeze.

Cancel Your Appointments

Before you install DoubleSpace, make sure you can afford the time it will need to compress the data on your hard disk. Each megabyte of data on your disk will take about a minute to compress. If you have a 60MB drive, the compression will take about an hour. When the compression is finished, DoubleSpace will *defragment* the compressed data using the MS-DOS Defrag program; that will take more time. Plus, it will take you 20 minutes or so to work your way through the Dblspace Setup program, reading all of its prompts and deciding how to answer its questions.

Installing DoubleSpace will take even more time if you follow my advice on precautions you should take beforehand. For example, you'll need to allow enough time to do a complete backup of your hard disk data before you begin. In all, you'll probably need an entire afternoon to safely install DoubleSpace.

Of course, you'll spend most of this time watching DoubleSpace work. You might be tempted to start DoubleSpace up before you leave the office for the day and let it run overnight. If you do that, though, be sure it is well underway before you leave. You don't want to come in the next morning only to discover that you needed to press the Enter key one more time to get things going.

Make a Plan

Before you install DoubleSpace, figure out the arrangement of compressed and uncompressed drives you want. Do you want to have a single compressed drive accessed as drive C? Or do you want to create two compressed drives, accessed as C and D, so that you can store program files on one and data files on the other to simplify your backup routine?

If your hard drive already has multiple partitions, you'll have to decide whether you want to combine them into one partition before you install DoubleSpace. If you're in that boat, refer ahead to Chapter 6, "Using More than One Compressed Drive," for advice on how to do that.

How much uncompressed disk space do you need? Certain types of files should be stored in uncompressed disk space. The *Microsoft Windows* permanent swap file is one common example of such a file. Certain copy protected programs should also be stored on an uncompressed drive.

When you install DoubleSpace, it usually leaves 2MB of free space on the host drive. DoubleSpace looks for a *Windows* permanent swap file and if it finds one, automatically moves it to uncompressed space on the host drive. You should increase the amount of free space left on the uncompressed host drive only if you have other specific files that need to be located in uncompressed disk space.

Back Up Everything

DoubleSpace's installation routine is designed to be safe. A DoubleSpace demonstration was a feature of Microsoft's announcement of MS-DOS 6.0 to the world. While DoubleSpace was in the middle of compressing the demonstration machine's data, Bill Gates himself reached underneath the table and unplugged the computer. I'm sure the entire DoubleSpace team back in Redmond was turning blue from holding its collective breath, but when Gates finally plugged the computer in again, DoubleSpace did just what it was supposed to do: it picked up right where it had left off and without missing a beat completed the data compression.

That ability to recover doesn't mean you shouldn't do a complete backup of your hard disk before you install DoubleSpace. It's good to know that DoubleSpace is as safe as safe can be. But circumstances are rarely perfect, and you'd be foolish to do something to your system as major as installing DoubleSpace without the safety net provided by a full backup.

Incidentally, whenever people tell me they're upgrading to MS-DOS 6 so that they can use DoubleSpace, I ask them if they'll have a tape drive handy to back up their newly doubled disk drive. It's bad enough trying to back up an 80MB disk drive to floppies. Once DoubleSpace has transformed the 80MB disk into a 160MB disk, backup to floppies is out of the question. A tape drive doesn't cost much more than the 100 or so floppies you'd need to back up a disk that large.

Do a Surface Scan (MS-DOS 6.0 Users Only)

If the surface of your disk drive contains a defect, the sector that's located at the defective location can't be read. When a disk drive is formatted, any sectors that can't be read are marked in the File Allocation Table as unusable. That way, MS-DOS won't try to write data to a cluster that contains an unreadable sector.

Unfortunately, disk defects can develop after the format, as you use your disk drive. MS-DOS doesn't dynamically detect these defects and mark them in the FAT, so there's always the possibility of your losing data by writing it to one of these bad clusters. When that happens, you won't be able to access the file the bad cluster is allocated to.

Because DoubleSpace is more efficient at using the sectors on your hard drive, it has an unfortunate tendency to uncover bad sectors that have escaped detection in ordinary disk use. Without DoubleSpace, a defective sector might sit around for months or even years without being discovered. Once you install DoubleSpace, the likelihood of that sector's being used shoots up. When DoubleSpace tries to write data to the bad sector, you'll have a serious problem.

ScanDisk in MS-DOS 6.2

Microsoft realized the potential for problems arising from using DoubleSpace on a drive that contained undiscovered bad sectors. With MS-DOS 6.2, they introduced a new utility program called *ScanDisk*, which scans the entire surface of your hard disk for defects. If ScanDisk finds a defect, it marks the bad sector in the FAT so that it won't be used. When you install DoubleSpace under MS-DOS 6.2, the DoubleSpace Setup routine automatically calls ScanDisk to do a surface analysis of your disk so that you can rest assured that DoubleSpace won't be tripped up by undetected bad sectors. We'll look at ScanDisk in more detail in Chapter 4, "Working with Compressed Data."

If you're using MS-DOS 6.0, I strongly suggest that you upgrade to 6.2 *before* you install DoubleSpace. Alternatively, you can use a third-party surface analysis program such as those in *PC Tools* and *The Norton Utilities* before you install DoubleSpace.

Defragment Your Disk

Next, run *Microsoft Defrag*, one of the new utility programs that comes with MS-DOS 6.0 and 6.2. Defrag cleans up your disk by eliminating *fragmentation*, a common condition in which the clusters that belong to files are jumbled up with clusters that are still available for use. Defrag moves all of your free clusters to the end of the drive and rearranges your files so that they can be accessed more efficiently.

The DoubleSpace Setup routine automatically invokes Defrag *after* it installs DoubleSpace and compresses your data. However, I still recommend that you run Defrag *before* you install DoubleSpace. It takes a little extra time to run Defrag first, but DoubleSpace installation can sometimes be tripped up by an excessively fragmented drive. It's best to eliminate fragmentation beforehand.

Check Your Disk Space

To compress the data on a disk, DoubleSpace needs to have a small amount of free space available on the disk. To compress your C drive, DoubleSpace needs at least 1.2MB of free disk space. To compress any other hard drive, it needs at least 1.1MB (650KB in MS-DOS 6.0 and 513KB in MS-DOS 6.2 for floppy disks) of free disk space.

To find out how much free disk space you have on your C drive, type *chkdsk*, with no parameters, at the C:\> prompt. Near the middle of the resulting report you'll see the amount of free space on the disk:

```
Volume DRIVE_C      created 02-23-1993 8:08p
Volume Serial Number is 1A57-A047

72214528 bytes total disk space
   73278 bytes in 2 hidden files
   30720 bytes in 12 directories
60555264 bytes in 386 user files
   61440 bytes in bad sectors

11493376 bytes available on disk
```

```
2048 bytes in each allocation unit
35261 total allocation units on disk
 5612 available allocation units on disk

655360 total bytes memory
619264 bytes free
```

In this case, the 72MB disk has just about 11MB of free space. That's more than enough free space for DoubleSpace to successfully compress the disk's data.

If Chkdsk reports less than 1.2MB of free space for your C drive or less than 1.1MB for any other hard drive (650KB in MS-DOS 6.0 and 513KB in MS-DOS 6.2 for floppy disks), you'll need to free up some disk space before you install DoubleSpace.

Fix Lost Clusters and Cross-Linked Files

If you're running MS-DOS 6.0 and Chkdsk reports any errors such as lost clusters or cross-linked files, you must fix them before you can install DoubleSpace. If Chkdsk says that you have lost clusters, rerun the Chkdsk command with the /f (for *fix*) switch:

```
C:\> chkdsk /f
```

Using Chkdsk with the /f switch creates a number of probably useless files in the drive's root directory named FILE0000.CHK, FILE0001.CHK, and so on. After checking that the files are unimportant, delete them with this command:

```
C:\> del file*.chk
```

If Chkdsk says that you have cross-linked files, note the names of the files that are cross-linked. Then, copy the cross-linked files to new files and delete the originals. This removes the cross-linked condition. However, since one or both of the files is likely to be unusable, you should probably delete them both and replace them with copies restored from a current backup. (You do have a current backup, don't you?)

If you're running MS-DOS 6.2 and Chkdsk reports lost clusters, cross-linked files, or other errors, fix them by running the ScanDisk command. (When ScanDisk asks whether you want to perform a surface scan, reply *No*. ScanDisk automatically performs a surface scan when you install DoubleSpace, so there's no point in doing one now.)

Check Your Memory

One big surprise to many unsuspecting DoubleSpace users is the discovery that DoubleSpace itself requires a large amount of memory: 43KB for MS-DOS 6.0 and 34KB or 38KB for MS-DOS 6.2, depending on how you configure DoubleSpace. This memory requirement can put a strain on systems whose memory is already packed full with memory resident programs and device drivers. You'd better find out beforehand whether you can afford the memory DoubleSpace will require.

The good news for users with 386 or better processors is that DoubleSpace can load high, into the area of memory between 640KB and 1MB called *Upper Memory*. And there's more good news: MS-DOS 6.0 and 6.2 include an improved version of EMM386.EXE that more than makes up for the extra memory required by DoubleSpace. The new EMM386.EXE does a more thorough job of searching out upper memory than the previous version did. As a result, it's able to access over 100KB more upper memory than the MS-DOS 5 version of EMM386.EXE did.

The bad news is that many users already knew that the MS-DOS 5 version of EMM386.EXE could be improved upon, so they bought a third-party memory manager such as QEMM-386 or 386MAX. If you use one of these memory managers, you've probably already recovered as much upper memory as the MS-DOS 6.0 and 6.2 version of EMM386.EXE can, possibly more. And you've probably already filled it up.

To find out for sure, all you have to do is type *mem* with no parameters. Mem will produce a report that details your memory usage. The next-to-the-last line of the report is the one you'll be interested in. It will show the largest block of free upper memory:

```
Largest free upper memory block    78K   (80,256 bytes)
```

As long as this line shows that you have a block larger than 43,504 bytes (MS-DOS 6.0) or 37,696 bytes (MS-DOS 6.2), you can install DoubleSpace without worrying about losing conventional memory to DoubleSpace.

If Mem shows that you don't have enough room for DoubleSpace, you should run the MS-DOS 6.0 and 6.2 Memmaker program to optimize your memory configuration. When Memmaker has finished, run Mem again to see if you now have enough memory for DoubleSpace. If you don't, you'll either have to remove a device driver or memory resident program from your CONFIG.SYS or AUTOEXEC.BAT file or put up with the loss of conventional memory.

Log On to the Network (if You Use One)

If your computer is attached to a network, be sure to log on to the network before you install DoubleSpace so that DoubleSpace will be aware of your network drive assignments. If you don't log on to the network before you install DoubleSpace, you might find yourself unable to access your network drives later.

HOW TO INSTALL DOUBLESPACE

DoubleSpace functions are accessed through the Dblspace command. The first time you type *dblspace*, the Dblspace program runs its setup routine to install DoubleSpace.

Starting DoubleSpace Setup

When you're ready to install DoubleSpace, follow these steps:

1. Type *dblspace* at the C:\> prompt. When you do, DoubleSpace Setup will display the welcome screen shown in Figure 3-1.

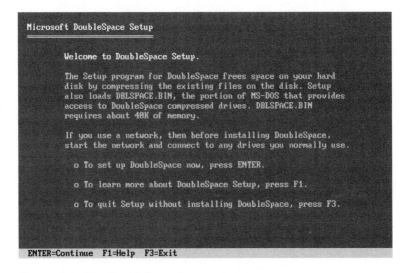

Figure 3-1. *The DoubleSpace Setup welcome screen.*

Read this screen over carefully to make sure you understand what you're doing. You can press F1 to display a brief explanation of how DoubleSpace Setup works.

2. When you're ready to continue, press the Enter key. DoubleSpace Setup will display the screen shown in Figure 3-2. This screen gives you the choice of Express Setup or Custom Setup.

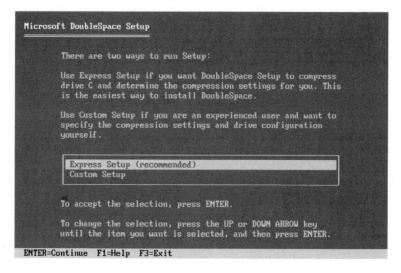

```
Microsoft DoubleSpace Setup


        There are two ways to run Setup:

        Use Express Setup if you want DoubleSpace Setup to compress
        drive C and determine the compression settings for you. This
        is the easiest way to install DoubleSpace.

        Use Custom Setup if you are an experienced user and want to
        specify the compression settings and drive configuration
        yourself.

        ┌──────────────────────────────────────────────────────┐
        │ Express Setup (recommended)                            │
        │ Custom Setup                                           │
        └──────────────────────────────────────────────────────┘

        To accept the selection, press ENTER.

        To change the selection, press the UP or DOWN ARROW key
        until the item you want is selected, and then press ENTER.

  ENTER=Continue  F1=Help  F3=Exit
```

Figure 3-2. *Selecting Express Setup or Custom Setup.*

You'll probably want to pick Express Setup, which will automatically compress the files on drive C. Custom Setup will let you compress the files on any drive, or it will let you create an empty compressed drive without actually compressing any files.

3. When you select Express Setup, DoubleSpace displays a screen similar to the one in Figure 3-3. This screen offers you your last chance to bail out of DoubleSpace Setup.

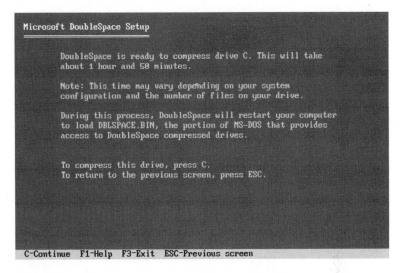

Figure 3-3. *DoubleSpace Setup offering you one last chance to bail out.*

This screen tells you which drive DoubleSpace is going to compress and estimates how long the compression will take.

If you're using MS-DOS 6.2, DoubleSpace politely warns you that you should back up your hard disk before you continue. You already did that, though. Right?

Compressing the Drive

When you press C to continue the installation process, DoubleSpace Setup takes the following steps:

1. In MS-DOS 6.0, DoubleSpace runs the Chkdsk program to make sure there are no errors in the disk's FAT and directory structures. In MS-DOS 6.2, DoubleSpace runs the ScanDisk program instead of Chkdsk. ScanDisk checks the disk surface for errors. Figure 3-4 on the next page shows ScanDisk at work.

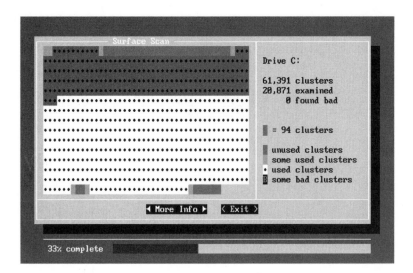

Figure 3-4. *ScanDisk reporting as it checks the disk surface for defects.*

2. Next, DoubleSpace makes adjustments to your CONFIG.SYS and
   AUTOEXEC.BAT files and reboots your computer. It adds a command to CONFIG.SYS to move DBLSPACE.BIN into upper
   memory (or to the bottom of conventional memory). It adds a temporary command to AUTOEXEC.BAT so that DoubleSpace Setup will
   be restarted where it left off if there should be a power failure and
   reboot. Don't worry. DoubleSpace restores AUTOEXEC.BAT to its
   original state when Setup finishes. The change to CONFIG.SYS is
   permanent.

3. As DoubleSpace compresses the drive, it displays its progress on a
   screen like the one shown in Figure 3-5. You can see how much
   more time DoubleSpace estimates the compression will take, which
   file is currently being compressed, and how much of the disk has
   already been compressed.

   This is the phase of DoubleSpace setup that takes about one minute
   per megabyte of data. DoubleSpace doesn't require your attention
   during this phase, so you don't have to sit around and watch the bar
   chart crawl across the screen at a snail's pace. Now's the time to go
   to lunch. If you have a really large disk drive, you might even
   squeeze in a round of golf.

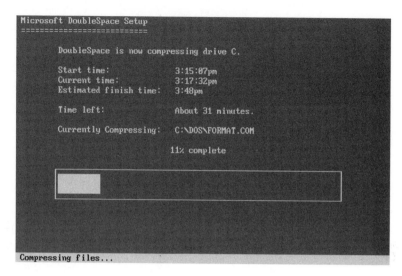

Figure 3-5. *DoubleSpace Setup displaying its progress.*

4. When DoubleSpace has finished compressing the drive, it invokes the Defrag program to optimize the compressed drive.

Success!

When DoubleSpace has been installed and your disk has been compressed, DoubleSpace displays a screen like the one in Figure 3-6.

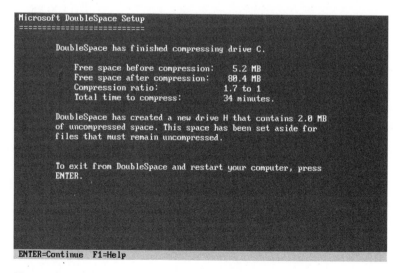

Figure 3-6. *DoubleSpace Setup bragging about its success.*

You can see the results of DoubleSpace's compression. In this case, the amount of free space on the drive jumped from 5.2MB to a whopping 80.4MB. The average compression ratio for all the files on the disk is 1.7 to 1. That's an average, so some files compressed at a better ratio, some not as well.

Notice that DoubleSpace says it created a new drive H that contains 2MB of uncompressed space. This is the host drive I told you about in Chapter 1. It would be a little more precise to say that DoubleSpace created a new compressed drive and then swapped the drive letters around so that the data on the new compressed drive can be accessed as drive C.

When you press the Enter key, DoubleSpace returns your CONFIG.SYS and AUTOEXEC.BAT files to their original states (except that the CONFIG.SYS file now contains the line that relocates DBLSPACE.BIN) and reboots your computer.

What About Custom Setup?

Express Setup is perfect if you have only one hard drive (drive C) and you want to compress all of it. It's also ideal if you have two or more hard drives and you want to start by compressing your C drive. You can then use the installed DoubleSpace program to manually compress the data on your other drives using the techniques you'll learn about in Chapter 6, "Using More than One Compressed Drive."

If you're a power user, you'll probably look into Custom Setup even if I tell you not to. That's the way we power users are. But prepare yourself for a surprise. You probably expect to find dozens of options and extras that aren't available to the novice user. Instead, you'll find that Custom Setup lets you do only three things that Express Setup doesn't:

■ Custom Setup lets you compress a drive other than C as you install DoubleSpace.

For example, if you have three hard drives (C, D, and E), Custom Setup lets you start by compressing drive D or E whereas Express Setup always compresses drive C. There's usually little reason to start with a drive other than C. You can always compress the other drives later.

■ Custom Setup lets you install DoubleSpace by creating an empty compressed drive rather than by compressing existing data.

If you choose this option, DoubleSpace will leave your existing files alone but will create an empty compressed drive using the free space on one of your existing drives. Using this Custom Setup option won't take nearly as much time as Express Setup because Setup won't have to compress any files. I recommend that you use this option only if you have more than 500MB of files on your hard drive. With that much data, DoubleSpace won't be able to fit everything on a single drive. The best way to handle this situation is to use Custom Setup to create an empty compressed drive and then copy as many files as will fit onto the drive. Then, compress the remaining files using the DoubleSpace Compress menu's Existing Drive command as described in Chapter 5.

In general, though, I don't recommend that you use the Custom Setup option to set DoubleSpace up this way. Some users set up DoubleSpace this way thinking that they'll be able to test drive it without committing their valuable data to it. But if you set up DoubleSpace this way, you'll eventually have to set it up right. And it's easier to set it up right if you do it right the first time.

■ Custom Setup lets you determine compression settings yourself.

The compression settings include the drive letters assigned to compressed drives, the compression ratio used to calculate the amount of free space remaining on the drive, and the amount of uncompressed space to leave on the host drive. Since you can change all of these variables later, I recommend that you let DoubleSpace use its defaults, which are sensible in most cases. You'll learn how to change the default compression settings in Chapter 4, "Working with Compressed Data."

WHAT TO DO *AFTER*
YOU INSTALL DOUBLESPACE

Whew! DoubleSpace Setup has finished without displaying any error messages, so you're all set, right? Not quite. You need to take care of a few details before you can pronounce DoubleSpace "installed."

Explore Your System

DoubleSpace has made a number of significant changes to your system. Do some exploring to find out exactly what those changes are.

■ Run Chkdsk on both the compressed drive and the host drive. Notice how much free space is available on both.

■ To look at the hidden files on the host drive, use the Dir /ah command. Notice how large the DBLSPACE.000 file is. This is the Compressed Volume File that contains all of the files on your compressed C drive.

■ If you want to see a list of all the drives on your system, run the Dblspace /list command. I'll explain the details of this command's output in Chapter 4, "Working with Compressed Data."

■ Use the Type command to see your CONFIG.SYS file, and notice that DoubleSpace has inserted a line similar to this one:

```
DEVICEHIGH=C:\DOS\DBLSPACE.SYS /MOVE
```

This line is required to place DoubleSpace in upper memory.

It's easier to explore some of these changes from the MS-DOS shell. When you start the MS-DOS shell, you'll notice that the host drive appears as an icon on the screen. To display the hidden and system files on drive H, from the File menu's Display Options command, choose the Display Hidden/System Files option.

Make Sure That
DBLSPACE.BIN Loaded High

If your computer has a 386 or better processor, you should run the Mem program to make sure that DBLSPACE.BIN successfully loaded into upper memory. Use the /c (for *classify*) and /p (for *pause*) switches:

```
C:\> mem /c /p
```

The /c switch causes Mem to display a detailed list of memory usage. The /p switch causes the display to pause between screens of output. The resulting output should look something like the output shown in Figure 3-7.

```
Modules using memory below 1 MB:

 Name            Total      =    Conventional  +   Upper Memory
 ---------       ---------       ------------      ------------
 MSDOS          17,037  (17K)      17,037  (17K)          0  (0K)
 HIMEM           1,168   (1K)       1,168   (1K)          0  (0K)
 EMM386          3,120   (3K)       3,120   (3K)          0  (0K)
 COMMAND         2,928   (3K)       2,928   (3K)          0  (0K)
 MOUSE          24,368  (24K)         272   (0K)     24,096 (24K)
 SETVER            704   (1K)           0   (0K)        704  (1K)
 DBLSPACE       39,360  (38K)           0   (0K)     39,360 (38K)
 SMARTDRV       29,024  (28K)           0   (0K)     29,024 (28K)
 SHARE           6,688   (7K)           0   (0K)      6,688  (7K)
 Free          684,736 (669K)     626,016 (611K)     58,720 (57K)

Memory Summary:

 Type of Memory      Total     =    Used    +    Free
 --------------      --------      --------     --------
 Conventional        655,360        29,344      626,016
 Upper               158,592        99,872       58,720
 Reserved            131,072       131,072            0
 Extended (XMS)    7,443,584     2,323,584    5,120,000
Press any key to continue . . .
```

```
 --------------      --------      --------     --------
 Total memory      8,388,608     2,583,872    5,804,736

 Total under 1 MB    813,952       129,216      684,736

 Largest executable program size        625,920    (611K)
 Largest free upper memory block         58,560     (57K)
 MS-DOS is resident in the high memory area.
```

Figure 3-7. *Finding DBLSPACE.BIN with the Mem command.*

Look down the list of module names until you find the DBLSPACE module, and then look across the line to make sure the 39,360 bytes (MS-DOS 6.2 version) used by DoubleSpace are listed in the Upper Memory column rather than in the Conventional column.

If DoubleSpace loaded into conventional memory rather than upper memory, run Memmaker to see whether it can squeeze DoubleSpace into upper memory. If it can't, you're the unfortunate victim of RAM Cram. You'll have to carefully evaluate every line in your CONFIG.SYS and AUTOEXEC.BAT files that loads a program into upper memory to see whether there's something you can do without; otherwise, you'll have to learn to live with the reduced conventional memory.

Make Sure That Everything Still Works

DoubleSpace is pretty well behaved, so it shouldn't interfere with any hardware or software you already have. Nevertheless, if you have any of the following on your system, you should check them out to make sure they're still working:

- Networks and network drive assignments
- RAM drives (created by the *Device=ramdrive.sys* command in your CONFIG.SYS file)
- CD-ROM drives
- Removable hard drives (SyQuest or Bernoulli)
- Tape drives
- Sound cards
- Scanners
- Fax/modem cards

Create a DoubleSpace Panic Disk

Every computer user should have a panic disk—a bootable floppy disk containing your favorite disk utilities that you can use to access your system if for some reason your hard disk becomes unbootable. After you install DoubleSpace, you'll need to create a DoubleSpace-aware panic disk. If you try to boot from your old non-DoubleSpace panic disk or from a disk that contains an earlier version of MS-DOS, you won't be able to access your compressed drives.

Here's how to create a DoubleSpace panic disk:

1. Format a floppy disk using the command Format /s. This format will copy COMMAND.COM and the system files IO.SYS, MSDOS.SYS, and DBLSPACE.BIN to the disk. The DBLSPACE.BIN file is what makes the system disk usable with DoubleSpace drives.

2. Copy your CONFIG.SYS and AUTOEXEC.BAT files to the disk.

3. Copy any other MS-DOS command files you might want to have available in the event that MS-DOS is completely unable to access your C drive. At the very minimum, copy FDISK.EXE and FORMAT.COM. The ATTRIB.EXE, CHKDSK.EXE, SCANDISK.* (6.2 only), and DBLSPACE.EXE files are also useful.

You should also make sure that you have a copy of your backup program on a floppy disk. You might need it to restore data from a recent backup.

SUMMARY

DoubleSpace is safe and easy to install if you know what you're getting into and you take a few precautions. The Express Setup option is ideal for most users.

- Allow plenty of time; don't install DoubleSpace in a hurry.

- Plan ahead how you want your DoubleSpace drives to be configured.

- Do a complete backup before you install DoubleSpace.

- If you're installing DoubleSpace in MS-DOS 6.0, use a disk utility such as *PC Tools* or *The Norton Utilities* to scan the surfaces of your disk for defects.

- Make sure you have at least 1.2MB of free disk space on your C drive and 1.1MB of free disk space on any other hard drive (650KB in MS-DOS 6.0 and 513KB in MS-DOS 6.2 for floppy disks) you plan to compress.

- Make sure you can afford the memory DBLSPACE.BIN will take up.

- Log on to your network so that DoubleSpace will know about your network drives.

- Type *dblspace* at the command prompt, and let Express Setup do the work for you.

- When DoubleSpace Setup is finished, check everything out to make sure it still works.

- Create a DoubleSpace-aware panic disk that contains the MS-DOS system files, DBLSPACE.BIN, and your favorite disk utilities.

Isn't that amazing?

— Dan Aykroyd, Saturday Night Live

Chapter 4

Working with Compressed Data

Now that you've installed DoubleSpace on your computer, you can forget about it and let it do its work with no further attention from you, right? Not quite. DoubleSpace is *mostly* transparent, compressing and decompressing data automatically whenever you or one of your programs accesses the disk. But DoubleSpace does introduce some subtle complications into your day-to-day PC life.

In this chapter, we'll take a look at those complications. Some of the complications arise from new command switches Microsoft introduced in MS-DOS 6.0 to support DoubleSpace drives. Others come from the presence of that pesky host drive: where you once had only one disk drive to contend with, you now have two (a compressed drive and a host drive).

You might already know that the Dblspace command has a truckload of switches that let you perform a number of functions for DoubleSpace drives. We'll get to those switches in later chapters. For now, let's focus on how DoubleSpace affects the way you use other MS-DOS commands.

USING CHKDSK (MS-DOS 6.0 ONLY)

Note: If you're using MS-DOS 6.2, most of the operations of the Chkdsk command have been superseded by the ScanDisk command. You'll still want to use the simpler Chkdsk command to check for the amount of free space on your disk, though.

If you're using MS-DOS 6.0, you use the Chkdsk command to check the logical structure of your hard disk. Chkdsk makes sure that the File Allocation Table and the root directory and other subdirectories agree with one another. If it discovers an error, it does its best to correct the error.

Note that Chkdsk does *not* check the physical reliability of your disk drive. If your drive's recording surface is developing defects, Chkdsk won't be able to discover and report them. All Chkdsk does is verify the integrity of your disk's FAT and directory structure.

If you haven't yet upgraded to MS-DOS 6.2, use the Chkdsk command periodically so that you can detect and fix structural errors as they develop. Many users put a Chkdsk command in the AUTOEXEC.BAT file. That way, the disk structure is checked every time they start their PCs.

When you use DoubleSpace, you will use the Chkdsk command twice as often: to check the structure of your compressed drives and of your host drives. If your compressed drive is C and your host drive is H, you should issue two Chkdsk commands:

```
C:\> chkdsk c:
```

and

```
C:\> chkdsk h:
```

Figures 4-1 and 4-2 show the output from these two commands.

ScanDisk in MS-DOS 6.2

Chkdsk's limits led Microsoft to introduce a new command, Scan-Disk, with MS-DOS 6.2. ScanDisk checks the logical structure of your disk more thoroughly than Chkdsk does, and it checks your disk's recording surface for defects. If you're using MS-DOS 6.2, you should use ScanDisk instead of Chkdsk to check your disk structure. We'll take up using ScanDisk in the section "Using ScanDisk (MS-DOS 6.2 Only)," later in this chapter. The only reason you'll continue to use Chkdsk is to get a quick display of the free space available on a compressed drive, the number of directories on the drive, and other disk information displayed by Chkdsk.

```
Volume DRIVE_C    created 02-23-1993 8:08p
Volume Serial Number is 1BD1-0A40

281903104 bytes total disk space
   180224 bytes in 14 hidden files
  2523136 bytes in 308 directories
253599744 bytes in 6773 user files
 25600000 bytes available on disk

     8192 bytes in each allocation unit
    38695 total allocation units on disk
     7408 available allocation units on disk

   655360 total bytes memory
   627168 bytes free
DoubleSpace is checking drive C.

DoubleSpace found no errors on drive C.
```

Figure 4-1. *Chkdsk output for a compressed drive.*

```
Volume HOST_FOR_C created 02-23-1993 8:08p
Volume Serial Number is 1A57-A047

170266624 bytes total disk space
164667392 bytes in 6 hidden files
  5599232 bytes available on disk

     4096 bytes in each allocation unit
    41569 total allocation units on disk
     1367 available allocation units on disk

   655360 total bytes memory
   619264 bytes free
```

Figure 4-2. *Chkdsk output for a host drive.*

Chkdsk Output for Compressed and Host Drives (MS-DOS 6.0 Only)

If you compare the output in Figures 4-1 and 4-2, you'll see some interesting differences between the compressed drive and the host drive. By comparing the total capacity of the compressed drive (281,903,104 bytes) with the total capacity of the host drive (170,266,624 bytes), you can see that DoubleSpace is able to create a 281MB disk drive in a CVF that's stored on a 170MB host drive. As Dan Aykroyd used to say, *Isn't that amazing?*

The Chkdsk output for the host drive shows that it contains more than 160MB of data in six hidden files. Nearly all of that data is stored in the Compressed Volume File (DBLSPACE.000). The five other files are the three system files (IO.SYS, MSDOS.SYS, and DBLSPACE.BIN), the DoubleSpace control file (DBLSPACE.INI), and the *Microsoft Windows* permanent swap file (386SPART.PAR).

The Chkdsk output gets more interesting when you compare the sizes of the clusters on the compressed and host drives. (Remember, the Politically Correct term for *cluster* is *allocation unit*.) The Chkdsk output for the host drive shows a cluster size of 4096 bytes—8 sectors are allocated for every cluster. The cluster size for the compressed drive is 8192 bytes, or 16 sectors for every cluster.

Didn't I say that DoubleSpace uses a *more* efficient method for allocating sectors to files? And isn't a larger cluster size *less* efficient than a smaller one? Yes to both questions. So what gives?

The secret here is that DoubleSpace doesn't really use 8192-byte clusters when it allocates space to your files. But it has to create the illusion that it does in order to stay compatible with as many existing MS-DOS programs as possible. So whenever MS-DOS or one of your programs asks DoubleSpace what its cluster size is, it tells a little white lie and politely says 8192.

In reality, DoubleSpace doesn't use all 8192 bytes for each cluster if it doesn't need them. If a given cluster needs only 4 sectors, DoubleSpace allocates just 4 sectors to that cluster. To keep track of how many sectors it has allocated to each cluster, DoubleSpace has to maintain a set of allocation tables on the disk in addition to the disk's standard File Allocation Table. If you're interested, you can read about these new allocation tables in Chapter 13, "Inside DoubleSpace."

Checking the Disk in MS-DOS 6.2

The MS-DOS 6.2 ScanDisk command checks the internal CVF structure directly, without calling Dblspace /chkdsk. In fact, the Dblspace program that comes with MS-DOS 6.2 doesn't even support the /chkdsk function.

Notice the last two lines of the output in Figure 4-1. When you run Chkdsk on a compressed drive, it verifies the FAT and directories as usual. Then, it invokes the Dblspace program to check the integrity of the new allocation tables used by DoubleSpace. In Chapter 5, "Using the Dblspace Program," you'll learn how to invoke this Dblspace /chkdsk function directly. But there's little reason to do that, since running the Chkdsk command checks both the standard FAT structure and the new CVF structure.

What Does It Mean, Spawn?

Two MS-DOS commands—Chkdsk and Defrag—do double duty when you use them with a DoubleSpace drive: after doing their usual work, they invoke the Dblspace command to perform a similar job on the compressed drive's CVF. When programmer types talk about Chkdsk's invoking Dblspace, they will often say, *Chkdsk spawns Dblspace /chkdsk.* What exactly do they mean when they say one program *spawns* another?

They mean that the first program uses a special MS-DOS function (Load and Execute Program) to invoke the second program. Because the first program is called the *parent program* and the second program is called a *child program,* the process is called *spawning.* When one program spawns another, the parent program is temporarily suspended while the child program runs. When the child program finishes running, the parent program picks up where it left off.

While the child program runs, it isn't aware that it's running under control of a parent program. It operates just as if you had started it up from the command line. The parent program provides any command-line arguments that are required. So when Chkdsk and Defrag spawn Dblspace, they provide the Dblspace switches necessary to invoke the correct function.

Fixing Errors with Chkdsk /f (MS-DOS 6.0 Only)

Chkdsk not only can detect errors in a disk's allocation tables, but it can also correct them if you use the /f switch, like this:

```
C:\> chkdsk /f
```

The two most common types of errors that can be detected by Chkdsk are lost clusters and cross-linked files. In Chapter 3, I briefly described how to use Chkdsk /f to fix these two types of errors.

When Chkdsk runs the Dblspace /chkdsk function to check the internal structure of the CVF, the /f switch allows it to fix any errors it finds in the CVF. So if Chkdsk reports any DoubleSpace errors, you can fix them with Chkdsk /f.

USING SCANDISK (MS-DOS 6.2 ONLY)

The Chkdsk command has been the primary MS-DOS tool for detecting and fixing disk errors since the introduction of hard disk support with MS-DOS version 2.0. Still, the Chkdsk command has a serious deficiency: it checks only the FAT and the directory structure of a hard disk; it can't check the physical reliability of a drive. With MS-DOS 6.2, Microsoft filled that deficiency by introducing a new command: ScanDisk.

ScanDisk does everything Chkdsk does, and more: it analyzes the FAT and the directory structure more thoroughly than Chkdsk; it corrects a greater range of error conditions; and it tests every sector of your hard disk to see whether there are any unreliable sectors. If there are, ScanDisk locks out those sectors so that MS-DOS won't allocate them to your files. If it can, it also moves any data that has been stored in the bad sectors so that you won't lose any files.

The ScanDisk command is intended to be a replacement for the Chkdsk command. In fact, if you run the Chkdsk command under MS-DOS 6.2, you'll receive the following message after Chkdsk's normal report of the disk capacity, free space, number of directories, and so on:

```
Instead of using CHKDSK, try using SCANDISK. SCANDISK can reliably detect
and fix a much wider range of disk problems. For more information,
type HELP SCANDISK from the command prompt.
```

Note that with MS-DOS 6.2, the Chkdsk command does *not* spawn the Dblspace /chkdsk function as it does in MS-DOS 6.0. The only way to verify the internal structure of a compressed drive under MS-DOS 6.2 is with the ScanDisk command. (However, the ScanDisk command doesn't display basic disk information such as the capacity of the disk, the free space on the disk, the number of directories on the disk, and so on. You may still need to use Chkdsk occasionally to display this information.)

ScanDisk Tips

- You can use the /all switch to tell ScanDisk to check all hard disk partitions and DoubleSpace drives:

  ```
  scandisk /all
  ```

  You can use /all and /custom together if you want to check all drives and avoid prompts.

- If you want ScanDisk to automatically correct errors without prompting you, use the /autofix switch:

  ```
  scandisk /autofix /nosummary
  ```

- If you want ScanDisk to just check your drive without correcting errors, use the /checkonly switch:

  ```
  scandisk /checkonly
  ```

- You can customize ScanDisk's operation by using the /custom switch:

  ```
  scandisk /custom
  ```

  Then, ScanDisk's actions are controlled by settings in a file named SCANDISK.INI, stored in your \DOS directory. If you want to explore this file, make a backup copy of it and edit it using the Edit command. It's a heavily commented file, so you should be able to figure out which ScanDisk functions the various settings control.

- If you have a Compressed Volume File that's so badly damaged DoubleSpace can't mount it, you might be able to fix it using ScanDisk. Just specify the CVF file name, instead of a drive letter, on the command line, this way:

  ```
  scandisk dblspace.000
  ```

How to Use ScanDisk (MS-DOS 6.2 Only)

1. At the MS-DOS command prompt, type *scandisk*. To check a specific drive, you can specify a drive letter:

   ```
   C:\> scandisk d:
   ```

   If you omit the drive letter, ScanDisk checks the current drive.

2. If the drive to be checked is a compressed drive, ScanDisk displays the screen shown in Figure 4-3.

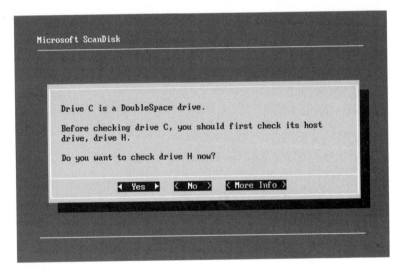

```
Microsoft ScanDisk


    Drive C is a DoubleSpace drive.

    Before checking drive C, you should first check its host
    drive, drive H.

    Do you want to check drive H now?

         ◀  Yes  ▶    ◀  No  ▶    ◀ More Info ▶
```

Figure 4-3. *ScanDisk's opening screen.*

Normally, you should choose Yes so that both the host drive and the compressed drive will be checked. (To select an option, click on the appropriate button with the mouse or press the first letter of the option name.)

3. ScanDisk displays the screen shown in Figure 4-4 as it checks the host drive.

   You can see from this screen that ScanDisk checks a variety of disk structures for the host drive.

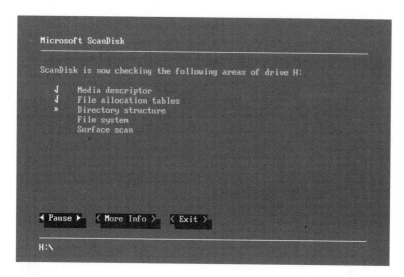

Figure 4-4. *ScanDisk as it checks the host drive.*

4. Because the surface scan can take awhile, ScanDisk doesn't run it automatically. Instead, it displays the screen shown in Figure 4-5 to ask if you want to do a surface analysis.

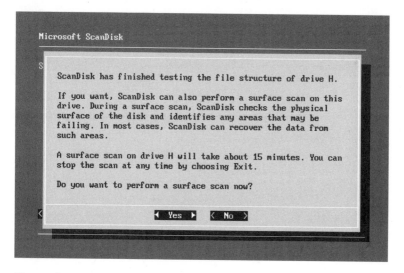

Figure 4-5. *ScanDisk asking whether you want to do a surface analysis of the disk.*

ScanDisk estimates how long the surface scan will take based on the size and speed of your disk drive and the speed of your computer.

5. During the surface scan, ScanDisk displays the progress screen shown in Figure 4-6.

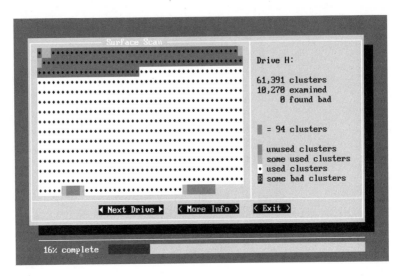

Figure 4-6. *ScanDisk as it analyzes the disk surface.*

In Figure 4-6, the left two-thirds of the screen is a *surface map* that represents the surface of your disk. The right third of the screen displays the progress of the scan and a legend that explains the symbols used to represent various elements of the disk surface. As ScanDisk scans each section of the disk, the corresponding symbol in the surface map changes color.

6. When ScanDisk finishes scanning the host drive surface, it checks the compressed drive, as shown in Figure 4-7. You can see that ScanDisk performs a few more checks for a compressed drive than it does for a host drive.

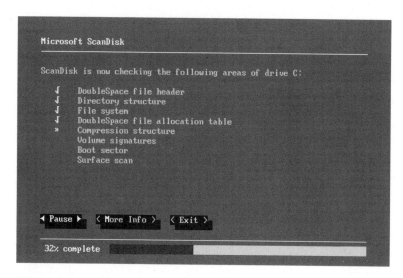

Figure 4-7. *ScanDisk checking the compressed drive.*

7. When ScanDisk is finished, it displays a summary screen like the one shown in Figure 4-8.

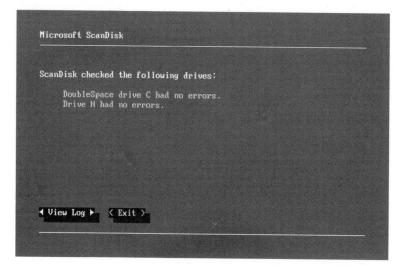

Figure 4-8. *ScanDisk reporting its results.*

Like Chkdsk, ScanDisk can fix errors it detects. In fact, ScanDisk does a more thorough job of fixing disk errors than Chkdsk does. You don't have to use the /f switch to get ScanDisk to fix an error. If ScanDisk detects an error, it displays a message that tells you in detail what the problem is and asks whether you want ScanDisk to fix it.

USING DIR

The Dir command works the same way for compressed drives as it does for uncompressed drives, with the exception of three new switches you can use for compressed drives: /c, /ch, and /oc.

The /c and /ch Switches

The /c and /ch switches tell Dir to display the compression ratio for each file. The subtle difference between the two lies in the way MS-DOS calculates the compression ratio. Figures 4-9 and 4-10 show output from the two switches.

```
C:\DOS>dir e*.* /c

Volume in drive C is MS-DOS_6
Volume Serial Number is 16EA-0958
Directory of C:\DOS

EMM386   EXE     120,926 09-30-93    6:20a    2.1 to 1.0
EXPAND   EXE      16,129 09-30-93    6:20a    1.0 to 1.0
EDIT     COM         413 09-30-93    6:20a   16.0 to 1.0
EDIT     HLP      17,898 09-30-93    6:20a    1.4 to 1.0
EGA      SYS       4,885 08-11-93    6:20a    2.0 to 1.0
EGA      CPI      58,870 09-02-93    6:20a    2.0 to 1.0
EGA2     CPI      49,090 09-02-93    6:20a    1.8 to 1.0
EDLIN    EXE      12,642 06-17-91    5:00a    1.5 to 1.0
EXE2BIN  EXE       8,424 06-17-91    5:00a    2.3 to 1.0
                1.9 to 1.0 average compression ratio
        9 file(s)       289,277 bytes
                     41,287,680 bytes free
```

Figure 4-9. *Dir /c output.*

```
C:\DOS>dir e*.* /ch

Volume in drive C is MS-DOS_6
Volume Serial Number is 16EA-0958
Directory of C:\DOS

EMM386   EXE    120,926 09-30-93   6:20a    2.1 to 1.0
EXPAND   EXE     16,129 09-30-93   6:20a    1.0 to 1.0
EDIT     COM        413 09-30-93   6:20a    8.0 to 1.0
EDIT     HLP     17,898 09-30-93   6:20a    1.2 to 1.0
EGA      SYS      4,885 08-11-93   6:20a    2.0 to 1.0
EGA      CPI     58,870 09-02-93   6:20a    1.9 to 1.0
EGA2     CPI     49,090 09-02-93   6:20a    1.8 to 1.0
EDLIN    EXE     12,642 06-17-91   5:00a    1.5 to 1.0
EXE2BIN  EXE      8,424 06-17-91   5:00a    1.7 to 1.0
            1.8 to 1.0 average compression ratio
      9 file(s)        289,277 bytes
                    41,271,296 bytes free
```

Figure 4-10. *Dir /ch output.*

MS-DOS calculates the compression ratio differently than you might expect it to. If a file that takes up 10,000 bytes uncompressed could be compressed to 5000 bytes, you'd expect the compression ratio to be 2.0 to 1.0.

But that's not how the calculation works. The compression ratio MS-DOS reports also takes into account the amount of space saved because of DoubleSpace's improved cluster allocation scheme. Let's look again at that 10,000-byte file. Since DoubleSpace always tells MS-DOS that it uses 8KB clusters, that file would actually require 2 clusters, or 16,384 bytes of disk storage, uncompressed. When DoubleSpace compresses the file to 5000 bytes, it can store it in 10 sectors, or 5120 bytes. Thus, the compression ratio is 16384/5120, or 3.2, to 1.0.

The difference between the /c and /ch switches is that /ch uses the cluster size of the host drive to calculate the compression ratio rather than the 8KB cluster size that's always used for the compressed drive. On my system, the host drive uses 4KB clusters. So that 10,000-byte file would require 3 clusters, or 12,288 bytes. Therefore, /ch would calculate the compression ratio for this file as 12288/5120, or 2.4, to 1.0.

Because of the way MS-DOS calculates compression ratios, Dir /c reports savings of 16.0 to 1.0 on very small files. For example, my 270-byte CONFIG.SYS file reports 16.0 to 1.0 compression with Dir /c. That's because the 270-byte file would require a full cluster, or 8192 bytes, in uncompressed form. Since DoubleSpace is able to store the file in a single sector, it reports a 16.0 to 1.0 savings (8192/512=16). The same file reports 8.0 to 1.0 compression with the /ch switch.

Which Is More Fair: /c or /ch?

The question of fairness often comes up when users compare the /c and /ch switches. If the /c switch consistently reports higher ratios than the /ch switch, it's natural to assume that the /ch report is probably the more accurate.

But it isn't necessarily. It depends on your point of view. If you're interested in the compression ratio for an individual file, use the /ch switch. It tells you how much a particular file was compressed compared with the way the file was stored before you installed DoubleSpace.

However, keep in mind that DoubleSpace has increased the capacity of your disk to the point at which you would probably have to use a larger cluster size. For example, before I installed DoubleSpace, MS-DOS used 4KB clusters on my 170MB disk. DoubleSpace expanded the capacity of my disk to about 280MB. But the largest disk drive MS-DOS can support with 4KB clusters is 256MB, so my disk's cluster size increased to 8KB. If I had bought a 280MB disk drive instead of using DoubleSpace, I would have had to use 8KB clusters anyway. In this case, the /c switch's use of 8KB clusters is entirely reasonable.

The only time /c truly overstates the compression ratio is when the size of your CVF is under 256MB. In that case, /c calculates compression based on an 8KB cluster size—when a smaller cluster size would be used on an equivalent uncompressed drive.

The /oc Switch

The Dir command's /oc switch lets you display a directory listing sorted according to the files' compression ratios. If you type

```
dir /oc
```

the directory listing will include the compression ratios as if you had specified /c and the files will be sorted into sequence with the smallest ratios first. To reverse the order, type

```
dir /o-c
```

and the files will be listed with the highest compression ratios first.

If you want to sort the listing by ratios calculated using the host cluster size, you must use /oc and /ch together:

```
dir /oc /ch
```

An Extreme Case

Can DoubleSpace compress a 1-byte file? To find out, create one by typing this command:

```
copy con onebyte.txt
```

Then, press the spacebar, Ctrl+Z, and the Enter key. Now type *dir onebyte.txt* and you'll see that the file contains just 1 byte. Now type *dir onebyte.txt /c* and you'll see that DoubleSpace has achieved a compression ratio of 16.0 to 1.0 for even a 1-byte file. Has it managed to compress the 8 bits of data in this file into half a bit?

No. This is just an extreme example of the benefits of Double-Space's improved space allocation scheme. With 8KB clusters, the 1-byte file took 16 full disk sectors. Since DoubleSpace allocates only one sector to this file, it reports a compression ratio of 16.0 to 1.0.

Even though DoubleSpace was not able to compress the data in this file (you can't compress a 1-byte file), it still managed to save 15,872 bytes of disk space. How significant is this savings? On average, the savings for every file on your disk will be half a cluster, or 4KB. On my hard disk, which has more than 6700 files, that adds up to well over 25MB of saved space.

Using Dircmd to Set Dir Defaults

If you'd like the Dir command to always display the compression ratio, add this command to your AUTOEXEC.BAT file:

```
set dircmd=/c
```

Then, whenever you use the Dir command, the /c switch will be added. You can add any combination of switches you want to this command. For example, to display files in file name order with compression ratios, add this command to AUTOEXEC.BAT:

```
set dircmd=/on/c
```

USING BACKUP

Don't.

USING MSBACKUP

DoubleSpace isn't the only cool new MS-DOS feature, of course. The old Backup command was getting pretty long in the tooth. It was fine when the largest disk drives were 10MB, but it's been pretty helpless against 100MB drives. Something had to be done.

Enter *Microsoft Backup,* the new MS-DOS backup program licensed from Symantec, the makers of *The Norton Backup* (and other great utility programs too). Microsoft Backup speeds backup by using a feature called *DMA* (for *Direct Memory Access*) to allow your drives to run at high speed and by compressing data as it is written to disk. Microsoft Backup uses the same compression routines as DoubleSpace.

This isn't the place for a complete tutorial on using Microsoft Backup. Fortunately, the program is easy enough to figure out once you get it started: just type *msbackup* and start exploring. If you get stuck, there are plenty of books available that present complete information about Microsoft Backup.

Our focus here will be on the procedure you should follow to back up data on a compressed drive. The question that naturally comes up is *Should you back up your compressed drive, your host drive, or both?* In most cases, the answer is that you need to back up the compressed drive but not the host drive. If for some reason you lose your hard drive, you can easily re-create the host drive manually. Then, you can create an empty compressed drive and restore the backup of your old compressed drive into it. You'll find instructions for doing that in Chapter 7, "Working with Compressed Floppies and Removable Drives."

If you backed up only your host drive and then lost an individual file, you wouldn't be able to restore just that one file. That's because your host drive contains the entire contents of your compressed drive in a single file: the CVF. There's no way to selectively restore just one file from a backup copy of the CVF.

I recommend that you use a combination of occasional full backups and regular incremental *or* differential backups to back up your compressed drive. How often you should back up depends on how frequently you use your PC and how important your files are to you. I back up every day because my livelihood depends on my computer files.

The difference between an incremental backup and a differential backup is subtle but important. An *incremental* backup is a backup of all the files that have changed since the last time you did a full or an incremental backup. A *differential* backup is a backup of all the files that have changed since the last time you did a full backup. If you work on the same small set of files day after day, you should opt for differential backups. If you work on different files each day, incremental backups are probably a better choice.

As for the host volume, you do need to back it up if it contains anything other than these files:

    IO.SYS
    MSDOS.SYS
    DBLSPACE.BIN
    DBLSPACE.INI
    DBLSPACE.000

If it does, use Microsoft Backup's Exclude Files feature to exclude the files listed above from the backup of the host volume. (If you have more than one compressed volume on a single host, use the wildcard file-spec *dblspace.0??* to exclude them all.) Then you can back up the rest of the files on the host drive.

Msbackup Tips

- Create a setup file for each drive you want to back up. In the setup file, specify an incremental or a differential backup. Then, whenever you do a full backup, change the backup type to full. This way, Msbackup will coordinate your full and incremental or differential backups using a catalog.

- When you run Msbackup, specify the setup file on the command line:

```
msbackup drive-c
```

  Here, *drive-c* is the name of the setup file.

- Make sure you've set the Compress Backup Data and Use Error Correction options. Set the Audible Prompts option if you want Msbackup to beep at you when it's time to insert a disk, and set Quit After Backup if you want Msbackup to quit when the backup is finished. All other Msbackup options should usually be off.

- If you're a *Microsoft Windows* user, use the *Windows* version of Microsoft Backup.

- If you know how, create a startup menu that lets you run Msbackup. You can do this with a batch file that uses the new Choice command, or you can use the MS-DOS shell.

- If you can possibly afford it, buy a tape drive. With the increased capacity of your DoubleSpace'd disk, you'll need it. You can buy tape drives that can hold up to 120MB per tape for around $150. Unfortunately, Microsoft Backup doesn't support tape drives, so you'll have to use the backup software that comes with the drive.

USING DEFRAG

Another new utility that comes with MS-DOS 6.0 and 6.2 is *Microsoft Defrag*. The Defrag utility addresses the common problem of excessive file fragmentation. A file is said to be *fragmented* when its clusters are not adjacent to one another on the disk. Fragmentation happens because whenever you create a new file, MS-DOS stores the file in the first open disk space it can find. If this space isn't large enough to hold all of the file, MS-DOS stores as much of the file as possible at that location and then finds the next open space for the next part of the file.

Fragmentation is itself not a serious problem. In fact, fragmentation can be thought of as an advantage. If MS-DOS didn't allow files to become fragmented, you wouldn't be able to create a new file unless you had enough free adjacent clusters to hold the entire file. With fragmentation, MS-DOS can make maximum use of all available disk space by tucking bits and pieces of files into every available nook and cranny of your disk.

There are drawbacks to fragmentation, however. It slows down disk access because the drive's read/write heads have to move to different disk locations to retrieve the file. And file fragmentation decreases the odds of recovering from problems such as lost clusters and cross-linked files. File fragmentation is an essential feature of MS-DOS, but it's best to minimize it as much as possible.

That's where Defrag comes in. It reorganizes all of the files on your disk so that fragmentation is eliminated. To use the Defrag command, just type *defrag* at the command prompt. Then, pick the drive you want to defragment. Defrag will analyze the drive to determine the amount of fragmentation, recommend a defragmentation method, and proceed to defragment your disk after you give it the go-ahead. (Defrag can defragment your drive using one of two methods: Full Optimization, which defragments your files and packs them together at the front of your drive so that all available free space is together at the end of your drive; and Unfragment Files Only, which defragments your files but doesn't consolidate the free space. Full optimization takes longer but is more thorough.) Figure 4-11, on the next page, shows Defrag in action.

Before you use Defrag on a DoubleSpace drive, take the time it eats up into account. Two types of fragmentation occur on a compressed drive. Because a compressed drive uses a File Allocation Table just as an uncompressed drive does, it can suffer from the kind of fragmentation I've just described. But a compressed drive can suffer from another type of fragmentation, called *sector heap fragmentation,* as well.

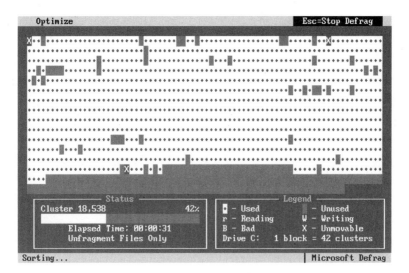

Figure 4-11. *Defrag in action.*

The *sector heap* is the part of the Compressed Volume File that contains the sectors allocated to your compressed files. DoubleSpace allocates sectors from the sector heap in a way that's completely unrelated to the way MS-DOS allocates clusters in the FAT. As a result, fragmentation can occur in the sector heap independently of fragmentation in the FAT.

Microsoft Defrag defragments the FAT, not the sector heap. When it has finished defragmenting the FAT, Defrag runs the Dblspace program to consolidate free space in the sector heap. Unfortunately, this consolidation is s-l-o-w. Hours-heaped-upon-hours slow. Let it work overnight.

Once you've defragmented your compressed drive, do you need to defragment your host drive too? Not usually. If the DoubleSpace CVF becomes excessively fragmented, you might need to defragment your host drive. The procedure, which is described in Chapter 8, "DoubleSpace Troubleshooting," is tedious.

Defrag Tips

■ You can bypass the Defrag prompts by specifying the drive and the optimization method you want on the command line. To defragment drive C using the full optimization method, use this command:

```
defrag c: /f
```

■ Defrag also lets you sort the files in your directories. To sort files into name sequence, add the switch /sn (for *sort* and *names*) to the command above:

```
defrag c: /f /sn
```

■ Defrag is designed to be restartable, so you don't have to worry about losing data if a power failure occurs while it runs.

■ Although there is a *Windows* version of Microsoft Backup, there is no *Windows* version of Defrag. Don't run Defrag while you're running *Windows*.

USING MSAV

MS-DOS 6.0 and 6.2 come with an antivirus program called *Microsoft Anti-Virus,* or *Msav.* Microsoft licensed this utility from Central Point Software, makers of *PC Tools.* Microsoft Anti-Virus scans your disk for viruses and removes any that it finds. In addition, you can use it to help prevent viruses from getting into your computer in the first place.

Msav doesn't really pose any special considerations for DoubleSpace use, but note that it doesn't automatically scan your DoubleSpace host drives. This omission creates a new opportunity for the wackos who create those sick virus programs, because many DoubleSpace users will diligently use Msav to scan their compressed C drives for viruses but will forget to scan their host drives.

So here's an important public service announcement: DON'T FORGET TO USE MSAV TO SCAN YOUR HOST DRIVE!

USING SMARTDRIVE

SMARTDrive speeds up the operation of your disk drives by creating a *disk cache* (pronounced *cash*), which works as a large buffer, large enough in some cases to hold thousands of disk sectors. SMARTDrive keeps recently accessed disk sectors in its buffer so that if they are needed again, they won't have to be read from disk. In addition, SMARTDrive anticipates which disk sectors your program is likely to need next so that it can read them in advance. Finally, SMARTDrive caches disk writes so that your program doesn't have to wait for the disk drive to complete a write operation before continuing.

Is SMARTDrive Safe?

You might have heard about problems associated with the write-caching feature of the MS-DOS 6.0 SMARTDrive program. Write-caching is an inherently risky proposition because it leaves data in a memory buffer while allowing you and your programs to assume that the data has been safely written to disk. A power failure or system reboot at the wrong moment could cause you to lose the cached data that hadn't yet been saved to disk.

Enough users complained about write-caching that Microsoft made it easier to disable in MS-DOS 6.2. When the MS-DOS 6.2 Setup program adds SMARTDrive to your AUTOEXEC.BAT, it configures it so that write-caching is disabled.

You can take some precautions to make the new version of SMARTDrive safe:

- Count slowly to five before turning off your PC. SMARTDrive never holds data in its cache for more than 3 seconds. If you allow a full 5 seconds of inactivity before turning off your PC, you won't leave any data stranded in the write cache.

- If you start your application programs from a batch file, add the following command to the batch file *after* the command that starts an application:

```
smartdrv /c
```

The MS-DOS 6.0 and 6.2 Setup program automatically adds a SMART-Drive command to your AUTOEXEC.BAT file, but you should check to make sure it's set up the way you want it to be. The only trick to setting up the SMARTDrive program for use with DoubleSpace is dealing with SMARTDrive's inability to cache compressed drives directly. Instead, SMARTDrive caches compressed drives indirectly, by caching the host drive that contains the CVF. This multiplies the benefit of the SMART-Drive cache because the data held in the cache will be compressed data. In other words, a 512KB cache can cache 1MB of data!

This command writes data held in the cache to disk. Then, you can trust that data will be written when you exit an application.

- If you have a batch file that contains a command that reboots your computer, insert a Smartdrv /c command before the reboot command.

- *Don't* worry about cached data when you restart your computer by pressing Ctrl+Alt+Del. SMARTDrive will detect this key sequence and write pending data to disk.

- *Do* worry about cached data when you turn off the power or press the Reset button. There is no way for SMARTDrive to detect either of these actions.

- If you've read all of this and write-caching still scares the willies out of you, disable it by editing the Smartdrv command in your AUTOEXEC.BAT file. Add drive letters for your floppy disk drives (A and possibly B), your DoubleSpace host drive, and any uncompressed hard drives:

```
smartdrv a b h
```

Or, if you're using MS-DOS 6.2, use the /x switch, this way:

```
smartdrv /x
```

The /x switch disables all write-caching.

If you don't specify any drive letters with the Smartdrv command, SMARTDrive caches read operations for all floppy disk drives and read and write operations for all hard drives, including DoubleSpace host drives. If you want to disable write-caching for a drive, you must specify its drive letter in the Smartdrv command—for instance:

```
smartdrv a b h
```

This command disables write-caching for drive H, which indirectly disables write-caching for any compressed drives hosted by drive H. This example of the command also lists the floppy disk drives A and B so that they will be read-cached too.

To disable caching for a drive altogether—both read and write—type a minus sign after the drive letter:

```
smartdrv a b h-
```

In this version of the command, drives A and B will be read-cached, but drive H (and any compressed drives hosted on it) will be neither read-cached nor write-cached. To enable both read- and write-caching for a specific drive, type a plus sign following the drive letter:

```
smartdrv a- b- h+
```

In this case, the floppy drives won't be read-cached but the H drive will be both read- and write-cached.

Note: If you don't specify any drive letters at all, the default for SMARTDrive is to read-cache floppy drives and read- and write-cache hard drives. However, if you specify any drive letters at all, you must specify all of the drives you want to be cached. In other words, if you specify just one drive letter, the default for any unspecified drive letters is no caching at all.

SUMMARY

For the most part, DoubleSpace doesn't affect the way you use MS-DOS and its commands. There are a few subtle considerations, however:

- You should run Chkdsk against both your compressed drives and your host drives.

- If you're using MS-DOS 6.2, you should use the ScanDisk command instead of Chkdsk.

- The Dir command lets you display compression ratios with the /c and /ch switches, and it lets you sort files into compression-ratio order with the /oc switch.

- The new Msbackup program is a big improvement over the old Backup command, but you should seriously consider buying a tape drive for backup if you're going to use DoubleSpace.

- Use Defrag to defragment your compressed drive, but expect DoubleSpace to take several hours to consolidate the free space in the sector heap of a Compressed Volume File.

- Don't forget to use Msav to scan your host drive as well as your compressed drives for viruses.

- Check the SMARTDrive command in your AUTOEXEC.BAT file to see if it's configured the way you want it to be. And make sure you're aware of the precautions you should take when write-caching is in effect.

We need...a nanny who can give commands!

— George Banks, *Mary Poppins*

Chapter 5

Using the Dblspace Program

The people who originally designed MS-DOS operated under a simple rule: for every function, there should be a command. George Banks, the tightly wound father in the children's classic *Mary Poppins*, would have loved MS-DOS. "Fancy that!" I can hear him saying, "a command for every occasion!"

For DoubleSpace, Microsoft tossed the one-command-for-every-function idea out the window. Instead, they took all the functions needed to keep DoubleSpace working spit-spot and combined them into a single command: Dblspace. What's more, they decided to make all of the command's functions available from easy-to-use menus! Supercalefragelisticexpialadocious! (There, I said it.)

This chapter is a gentle introduction to the Dblspace program. We'll survey its functions, and we'll look at how to use some of the more common functions. We'll look at other Dblspace functions in later chapters.

Command-line lovers, have no fear. All of the Dblspace command's functions are also available via command-line switches—you can access the functions directly without going through the menus. And you can incorporate the commands into batch files if you want to. As I show you how to invoke a Dblspace function by means of the menus, I'll also give you the equivalent command-line version with its switches. You'll find a complete reference to the Dblspace command in the appendix, "Dblspace Command Summary."

THE DBLSPACE PROGRAM

Now that you've installed the Dblspace program, you have a command center from which you can manage DoubleSpace drives.

1. To start the Dblspace program, just type *dblspace* at the command prompt. If you get a *Bad command or file name* message, change to the \DOS directory (or whatever directory you store your MS-DOS files in) and try again.

2. Once in Dblspace, you can activate Dblspace function menus by clicking on them with the mouse, provided you loaded the mouse driver before starting Dblspace. If you have a mouse but it doesn't work when you run Dblspace, add a MOUSE command to your AUTOEXEC.BAT file.

The Dblspace Opening Screen

Figure 5-1, on the next page, shows the screen Dblspace displays when you start it up.

Dblspace and the Keyboard

You can also invoke Dblspace functions by means of the keyboard.

- To activate a menu, hold down the Alt key and press the first letter of the menu name. When the menu appears, you can choose a command by using the arrow keys to select the command and pressing the Enter key or by pressing the letter that's highlighted in the command you want to use.

- To access the Dblspace online help, press F1.

- To exit Dblspace, press Alt+D and E then X.

- You'll find additional information about Dblspace in the MS-DOS help facility. Just type *help dblspace* at the MS-DOS command prompt.

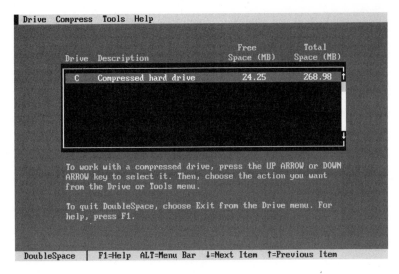

Figure 5-1. *The Dblspace program screen.*

In the center of the screen is a list of all your compressed drives. In this case, since I have only one compressed drive, there's only one entry in the list. If you have more than one compressed drive, you can use the arrow keys to select the compressed drive you want to work with. Notice that the list does have a scroll bar. If you're crazy enough to create more compressed drives than can fit in the box, you can access them all by scrolling.

For each drive, Dblspace displays this information:

■ The drive letter.

■ A description of the drive. In this case, the drive is a compressed hard drive. The description could also indicate that the drive is a compressed floppy disk or removable drive.

■ An estimate of the amount in megabytes of free space available on the compressed drive. To calculate this estimate, Dblspace must anticipate what the compression ratio for new files will be. If the new files you add to your drive compress better than the estimate predicts, you'll have more free space than the estimate indicates. If they compress worse than the estimate predicts, you'll have less free space than you think you do. You'll see in a moment how you can alter the ratio Dblspace uses to estimate the free space.

- The total capacity in megabytes of the compressed disk. Dblspace calculates the total capacity by adding the uncompressed size of all the files on the disk to the estimated free space remaining. As a result, the total capacity of the disk is also an estimate, based on an assumption about the compression ratio that will be achieved for files added to the disk.

The Dblspace Menus

Across the top of the initial Dblspace screen is a menu bar that contains four menus:

- The Drive menu lets you perform various functions for compressed drives. Use this menu to display information about a drive, to change the size or the compression ratio for a drive, to mount or unmount a compressed floppy disk, to format or delete a compressed drive, and to exit the program.

- The Compress menu lets you create new compressed drives. Its commands can either compress existing data or create an empty compressed drive. We'll reserve our closer look at the Compress menu for Chapter 6, "Using More than One Compressed Drive."

- For MS-DOS 6.0, the Tools menu includes two DoubleSpace functions that are best handled by stand-alone MS-DOS commands: Defragment and Chkdsk. The Tools menu also provides access to an Options dialog box that lets you change two options, the highest drive letter available for DoubleSpace use and the number of removable drives you want DoubleSpace to compress. (A "high" drive letter is one that comes late in the alphabet. Z is high; A is low.)

  For MS-DOS 6.2, the Tools menu also includes an Uncompress function, and the Options dialog box includes options to enable or disable the Automount and DoubleGuard features.

- The Help menu lets you access the Dblspace help system. You can also get context-sensitive help at any time by pressing F1.

THE DRIVE MENU

Figure 5-2 shows the Dblspace Drive menu. We'll look at the Drive menu's first three commands in this chapter. You'll learn about its other commands in later chapters.

Figure 5-2. *The Dblspace Drive menu.*

The Info Command

The Drive menu's Info command, as its name suggests, displays information about a compressed drive. To use it, first use the arrow keys at the Dblspace opening screen to select the drive whose information you want to display. Then, choose the Drive menu and the Info command with the mouse, or press Alt+D and then I.

When you choose the Info command, Dblspace displays drive information such as the information shown in Figure 5-3.

Dblspace /info

From the command prompt, you can display the information that appears when you use the Drive menu's Info command by typing:

```
dblspace /info c:
```

The /info switch is optional, so you can omit it:

```
dblspace c:
```

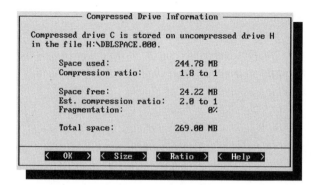

Figure 5-3. *The Info command screen for compressed drive information.*

You can learn a lot about your compressed drive from this display:

■ The host drive for this compressed volume is drive H.

■ The Compressed Volume File used for the compressed drive is named H:\DBLSPACE.000.

■ The compressed drive contains 244.78MB's worth of compressed data. That's the amount of disk space that would be required to store the files if they were uncompressed, not the actual amount of disk space required to store the files in compressed form.

■ The average compression ratio for all of the files on the drive is 1.8 to 1.

■ The estimated free space on the drive is 24.22MB.

■ The fragmentation is 0 percent (MS-DOS 6.2 only).

■ The free space is estimated assuming a compression ratio of 2.0 to 1 for any new files.

■ The estimated total capacity of the drive is 269.00MB. That just happens to be (not coincidentally) 244.78+24.22.

The Change Size Command

The Drive menu's Change Size command lets you change the size of the compressed drive. DoubleSpace does that by changing the size of the Compressed Volume File, but the way it changes the size of the CVF is a little backwards. Instead of telling DoubleSpace how big you want the compressed drive to be, you tell it how much free space you want to leave on the host drive. DoubleSpace then adjusts the size of the compressed

drive's CVF accordingly. Figure 5-4 shows the dialog box displayed by
the Change Size command.

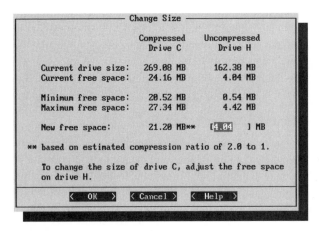

```
┌──────────────── Change Size ────────────────┐
│                                              │
│                    Compressed   Uncompressed │
│                    Drive C      Drive H      │
│                                              │
│  Current drive size:   269.08 MB   162.38 MB │
│  Current free space:    24.16 MB     4.04 MB │
│                                              │
│  Minimum free space:    20.52 MB     0.54 MB │
│  Maximum free space:    27.34 MB     4.42 MB │
│                                              │
│  New free space:        21.20 MB**  [4.04  ] MB │
│                                              │
│ ** based on estimated compression ratio of 2.0 to 1. │
│                                              │
│    To change the size of drive C, adjust the free space │
│    on drive H.                               │
│                                              │
│       <   OK   >    < Cancel >    <  Help  > │
└──────────────────────────────────────────────┘
```

Figure 5-4. *The Change Size command screen for changing the size of
a compressed disk.*

Dblspace /size

You can easily change the size of a compressed drive from the command line. In fact, it's more straightforward to change the compressed drive size from the command line because at the command
line Dblspace lets you specify the size of the CVF directly rather
than forcing you to think backwards by specifying the amount of
free space to leave on the host. To change the size of a compressed
drive's CVF to 100MB, use a command like this one:

```
dblspace /size=100 c:
```

If you *want* to specify the amount of free space to leave on the host
instead of the new size of the CVF, use a command like this one:

```
dblspace /size /reserve=10 c:
```

Here, I changed the size of drive C so that 10MB of free space is left
on the host drive.

Pop quiz: do the previous commands increase or decrease the size of
the compressed drive? Answer: you can't tell; it depends on how
much free space was on the host drive to start with.

The box shows you a lot of information, but DoubleSpace lets you change only one field: the New Free Space for the host drive field—in this example, Uncompressed Drive H.

- If you were to *increase* the amount of free space left on the host, DoubleSpace would *decrease* the space allocated to the CVF, which in turn would decrease the size of the compressed drive.

- If you were to *decrease* the amount of free space left on the host, DoubleSpace would *increase* the space allocated to the CVF, which in turn would increase the size of the compressed drive.

- Increasing the size of a compressed drive is called *growing* the drive. Decreasing the size of a compressed drive is called *shrinking* the drive.

- There are limits to how much you can grow or shrink a compressed drive. You can grow a compressed drive only until the amount of free space on the host gets down to about .5MB. And the amount by which you can shrink a compressed drive is limited by the data that's stored in the CVF. DoubleSpace displays these limits in the Minimum Free Space and Maximum Free Space fields for the host drive.

- As you adjust the value in the New Free Space field for the host, DoubleSpace recalculates the other values on the screen. That way, you can see what effect your changes will have.

If you have only one compressed drive and you don't need to store uncompressed files in the free space on your host drive, you probably won't use the Change Size command very often. As you'll learn in Chapter 6, "Using More than One Compressed Drive," the Change Size command is more useful when you have more than one compressed drive.

The Change Ratio Command

The Drive menu's Change Ratio command lets you change the compression ratio DoubleSpace uses to estimate the amount of free space available on the drive. Figure 5-5, on the next page, shows the Change Compression Ratio dialog box.

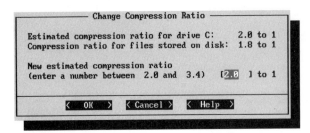

Figure 5-5. *The Change Ratio command screen for changing a drive's compression ratio estimate.*

As you can see, the dialog box displays the current compression ratio used to estimate free space and the actual compression ratio that has been achieved for files so far. Then, it lets you enter a new ratio.

When you change the compression ratio for a drive, the free space and total disk space will be changed to reflect the new ratio. Be clear on the difference between the Change Size and Change Ratio commands—both can change the free space and total capacity of the drive as reported by DoubleSpace:

- The Change Size command changes the size of the CVF used to hold a compressed drive. When you use the Change Size command, you actually change the amount of disk space available to the compressed drive.

- The Change Ratio command doesn't actually change the amount of disk space available to the compressed drive. Instead, it changes the estimate of how efficiently DoubleSpace will be able to use the space that is available to it. If your estimate isn't accurate, the free space and total capacity reported by DoubleSpace won't be accurate either.

Shouldn't you always set the estimated compression ratio to the actual compression ratio achieved for the files already on the disk? Not necessarily. On many compressed drives, the majority of files are program files, which don't yield outstanding compression statistics (usually 1.5 to 1 or so). Once you've compressed these files, it's likely that most of the new files you add to your disk will be data files, which will compress better.

The compression ratio for the files already on your compressed drive is thus probably not an accurate predictor of the compression ratio for new files.

It's usually safe to leave your estimated compression ratio set at 2.0 to 1.

Dblspace /ratio

To change the estimated compression ratio for a drive from the command line, use a command like this one:

```
dblspace /ratio=2.5 c:
```

This command changes the estimated compression ratio for drive C to 2.5 to 1.

If you want to change the estimated ratio to the actual ratio achieved for the files already on the drive, omit the number from the /ratio switch:

```
dblspace /ratio c:
```

You can change the ratios for all compressed drives with a single command. To do that, just specify the /all switch this way:

```
dblspace /ratio /all
```

THE TOOLS MENU

Figure 5-6 shows the Tools menu, which has several commands.

Figure 5-6. *The Dblspace Tools menu.*

Defragment and Chkdsk correspond to the DoubleSpace functions performed when you use the MS-DOS Defrag and Chkdsk commands. Since you're almost always better off performing these functions using their MS-DOS equivalents, I won't discuss them further here. See Chapter 4, "Working with Compressed Data," for discussions of using the MS-DOS commands Defrag and Chkdsk with compressed data. See Chapter 10, "Removing DoubleSpace," for a discussion of using the Uncompress command, which appears on the Tools menu in version 6.2.

The Options Command

Figure 5-7 shows the dialog box displayed by the Tools menu's Options command.

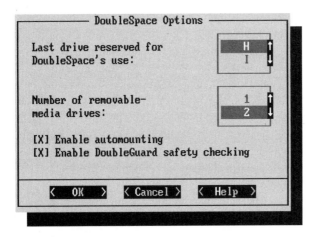

Figure 5-7. *The Options command screen.*

The Options dialog box lets you set two options that affect the way DoubleSpace works. Both of these options are a bit esoteric, so you're unlikely to need to change them.

The first option specifies the highest drive letter that's available for use by DoubleSpace. (Z is "higher" than A.) Usually, you should leave this option set to its default. If you find yourself creating lots of compressed drives and you run out of drive letters, you'll need to increase this setting.

The second option specifies the number of removable compressed drives—compressed floppy disks or removable cartridge drives such as

Bernoulli or SyQuest drives—you want DoubleSpace to handle. You should set this option to the number of removable drives you have. If you have two floppy disk drives, for instance, set this option to 2.

The third and fourth options are available only if you're using MS-DOS 6.2. These options let you enable or disable the Automount and DoubleGuard features.

THE DBLSPACE /LIST COMMAND

Throughout this chapter, we've seen how to use Dblspace command-line functions that are equivalent to the commands that appear on the Dblspace menus. One Dblspace command-line function has no menu equivalent: Dblspace /list. The Dblspace /list command displays a map of all of the drives recognized by DoubleSpace, as the example in Figure 5-8 does.

```
Drive  Type                       Total Free  Total Size  CVF Filename
-----  -------------------------  ----------  ----------  --------------
  A    Removable-media drive      No disk in drive
  B    Removable-media drive      No disk in drive
  C    Compressed hard drive        32.90 MB    378.71 MB  H:\DBLSPACE.000
  D    Available for DoubleSpace
  E    Available for DoubleSpace
  F    Available for DoubleSpace
  G    Available for DoubleSpace
  H    Local hard drive             15.24 MB    239.81 MB

DoubleGuard safety checking is enabled.
Automounting is enabled for drive(s) AB
```

Figure 5-8. *Output from the Dblspace /list command-line command.*

This list shows the total free space and the total capacity of all compressed drives and host drives, the CVF file names for all compressed drives, and the drive letters that are available for future use by DoubleSpace. (The DoubleGuard and Automount status lines are displayed only in Double-Space for MS-DOS 6.2.)

The benefit of the Dblspace /list output might not be apparent to you now, but if you have more than one hard drive or end up creating more than one compressed volume, Dblspace /list can be an invaluable tool for figuring out what's what.

SUMMARY

Dblspace is the command post for all DoubleSpace functions.

■ The Drive menu's Info command displays information about a particular compressed drive. The equivalent command-line switch is /info.

■ The Drive menu's Change Size command lets you change the size of a compressed drive, although you change it in a backwards-seeming way. The equivalent command-line switch is /size.

■ The Drive menu's Change Ratio command lets you change the compression ratio DoubleSpace uses to estimate the free space remaining on a compressed drive. The equivalent command-line switch is /ratio.

■ The Tools menu's Options command lets you specify which drives are reserved for DoubleSpace's use and how many removable drives DoubleSpace should support. In MS-DOS 6.2, you can enable and disable Automount and DoubleGuard. There is no command-line switch equivalent to the Options command.

■ The Dblspace /list command displays a mapping of compressed drives, host drives, and drives available for DoubleSpace use.

So double was his pains,
So double be his praise.

—Edmund Spenser, *The Faerie Queen*

Chapter 6

Using More than One Compressed Drive

So far in this book, we've looked at just the simplest of DoubleSpace set-ups: a single compressed drive and a single host drive. That's the configuration you'll have after you use Express Setup to compress your C drive. DoubleSpace provides for configurations much more complicated than that, however. In fact, DoubleSpace will let you create as many as 255 compressed drives. You'd be crazy to use that many, but you might well want to create two or three. And if you have more than one hard drive on your system, you can use each of them as a host drive.

DOUBLESPACE CONFIGURATIONS

DoubleSpace lets you set up more than one compressed drive on a single host, as shown in Figure 6-1.

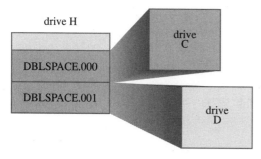

Figure 6-1. *A host drive with two compressed volumes.*

Here, I've set up two compressed drives (C and D) on my uncompressed host drive (H). To do this, DoubleSpace simply creates two Compressed

Volume Files on drive H. The CVF for drive C is named DBLSPACE.000; the CVF for drive D is named DBLSPACE.001. If you created a third compressed drive on the same host, its CVF would be (you guessed it) DBLSPACE.002.

Why would you want to set up two compressed drives instead of one? One good reason is to simplify your backup procedures. If you put all of your program files on compressed drive C and your data files on compressed drive D, you'll have to regularly back up only the files on drive D. You'll have to back up the files on drive C only when they change substantially—when you install a new program, for instance.

Another good reason to set up more than one compressed drive is an un-usually large hard drive. DoubleSpace limits the capacity of a single com-pressed drive to 512MB. If your hard drive is larger than 256MB, you can probably store more than 512MB of compressed data on it. But to do that, you'll have to create more than one compressed drive.

If your computer has two hard drives (or a single hard drive divided into two partitions), you can set up a compressed drive on each of them, as Figure 6-2 shows.

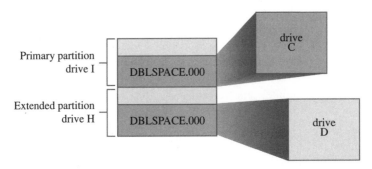

Figure 6-2. *Two host drives, each with a compressed volume.*

Here, each host drive is assigned a separate drive letter, so the host drive for compressed drive C is drive I, and the host drive for compressed drive D is drive H.

We'll look at how DoubleSpace assigns drive letters to compressed drives and host drives in arrangements such as these later in this chapter.

Get Rid of That Extended Partition!

If your hard drive uses an extended partition with logical drives, you might want to consider eliminating the extended partition and instead creating two or more compressed drives on the primary partition. Why? Because multiple compressed drives have a compelling advantage over multiple partitions: you can easily change their sizes. To change the size of a partition, you have to back up the files on the partition, run Fdisk to change the partition sizes, format the partitions, and restore the backup. But as you learned in Chapter 5, you can change the size of a compressed drive simply by using the Dblspace Drive menu's Change Size command.

Converting your configuration from a multiple partition setup to a single partition setup with multiple compressed drives can be tricky. It's easiest if you do it *before* you install DoubleSpace. Here's the procedure:

1. Back up *everything*—all of the data on all of your drives. Make sure you have a copy of your backup program on a floppy disk.

2. Use Fdisk to remove the extended partition and increase the size of the primary partition so that it fills the drive: type *fdisk* at the command prompt, and then delete all logical drives, the extended partition, and the primary partition; then create a new primary partition that fills the entire drive.

3. Reboot your computer, and reinstall MS-DOS and your backup program.

4. Restore the C drive backup to the enlarged primary partition.

5. Install DoubleSpace to compress your C drive, and set up the host drive as described in Chapter 3.

6. Use the Dblspace command to create a new compressed D drive on the same host. Make it at least as large as your old logical D drive.

7. Restore the backup of your old D drive to the new compressed D drive. The data will be compressed as it is restored.

8. Repeat the last two steps for each of your other old logical drives.

You can also combine the two types of configurations we've seen in Figures 6-1 and 6-2 if you want to. For example, if you have two hard drives, you could set up two compressed drives on each. In that case, you might have compressed drives C and E hosted on drive I and compressed drives D and F hosted on drive H.

THE COMPRESS MENU

To create a new compressed drive, you use the Compress menu, which is shown in Figure 6-3.

Figure 6-3. *The Dblspace Compress menu.*

As you can see, this menu has two commands: Existing Drive and Create New Drive.

- You use the Existing Drive command to compress data on a drive you haven't yet compressed. This command creates a compressed drive by compressing the existing files on the drive and moving them into a new compressed drive. You can use this command only once on each hard disk partition.

- You use the Create New Drive command to create an empty compressed drive. You can create as many empty compressed drives as you want on each hard disk partition.

  If you're like most users, you'll compress the existing data on your C drive when you install DoubleSpace. Then, to create additional compressed drives, you'll use the Create New Drive command.

CREATING AN EMPTY COMPRESSED DRIVE

To create a second compressed drive on an already existing host drive once you've installed DoubleSpace, you use the Compress menu's Create New Drive command after you're sure you've logged on to your network:

1. Start the Dblspace program by typing *dblspace* at the MS-DOS command prompt. Then, from the Compress menu choose the Create New Drive command. As in the example shown in Figure 6-4, Dblspace will display a list of the host drives that can accommodate a new compressed drive.

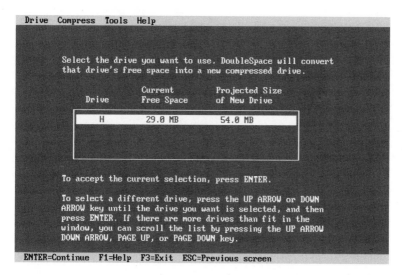

Figure 6-4. *The list of host drives summoned up by the Compress menu's Create New Drive command.*

For each host drive, Dblspace lists the amount of free space currently on the drive and the projected size of the new compressed drive, based on the default compression ratio, 2.0 to 1. (The projected size calculation reserves 2MB of free space on the host drive.)

2. If you don't have a host drive with enough free space to accommodate a new compressed drive or if you want the new drive to be larger than the estimate shown by Dblspace, press the Esc key to exit the Create New Drive command. Then, use the Drive menu's Change Size command to change the size of another compressed drive that resides on the same host, as described in Chapter 5. This will free additional space on the host drive. When you've finished, select the Create New Drive command from the Compress menu again and proceed.

3. If more than one host drive appears in the Create New Drive screen, select the one on which you want to create the new drive and then press the Enter key. Dblspace will display the compression settings for the new drive as in the example shown in Figure 6-5.

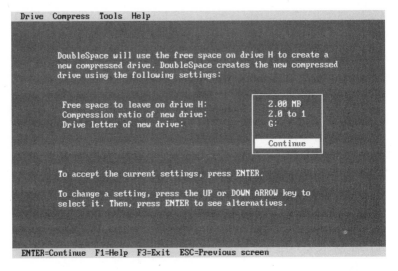

Figure 6-5. *The Create New Drive command's display of the default compression settings for the new compressed drive, offering you a chance to change the settings.*

This screen shows the default options for the new compressed drive: 2.0MB of free space will be left on the host drive, the estimated compression ratio for the new drive will be 2.0 to 1, and the new drive's drive letter will be G.

4. To change the size of the new drive, change the setting for the amount of free space that will be left on the host drive. Remember that each additional 1MB of free space you leave on the host drive reduces the size of the new compressed drive by 2MB (assuming you don't change the compression ratio).

5. If you expect that the data you will store on the new compressed drive will compress at a better ratio than 2.0 to 1, you might want to change the compression ratio setting. Remember that this ratio is used to estimate the amount of free space on the drive, so it needs to be as accurate as possible.

Making Sense of DoubleSpace Drive Letters

The default sequence in which DoubleSpace assigns letters to compressed drives and host drives can be confusing, but it does make sense when you understand the rules DoubleSpace follows when it conjures up those drive letter assignments:

- When you install DoubleSpace, it takes an inventory of your drive letter assignments. DoubleSpace realizes whether you have just one hard drive (C) or two or more. DoubleSpace is also aware of network drives if you log on to the network before you install DoubleSpace.

- DoubleSpace leaves four unused drive letters between your highest hard drive letter (usually C) and the drive letter it assigns to the first host drive. If you have just a C drive, the host drive letter is H—five letters past C. If you have a C and a D drive, the first host drive letter is I—five letters past D.

- Here's the tricky part. When you create additional DoubleSpace host or compressed drives, DoubleSpace assigns drive letters *backwards* from the host drive letter (H in our example). If the host drive letter is H, DoubleSpace assigns new compressed drive letters in this order: G, F, E, and D.

- Suppose you have two hard disks (drives C and D) and you compress drive C when you install DoubleSpace. DoubleSpace uses I for the host drive letter—five letters beyond the highest drive letter. If you next compress drive D, the host for drive D will be H, the next available drive letter below I.

- On the other hand, suppose you want to create three compressed drives on a disk that's divided into two partitions, C and D. First you compress drive C. DoubleSpace assigns drive letter I to the host for the compressed C drive. Next, you create a second, empty, compressed drive on the same host, I. DoubleSpace assigns this new compressed drive letter H. Finally, you compress drive D. DoubleSpace assigns drive letter G to the host for the compressed D drive.

6. You'll probably want to change Dblspace's suggestion for the drive letter to be assigned to the new compressed drive. Most of us expect drive letters to be in consecutive order starting with C (C, D, E, and so on). But Dblspace assigns compressed drive letters *backwards* from the host drive letter. So if the host drive letter is H, Dblspace will assign the letter G to the first new compressed drive you create, F to the next, and so on. Very disconcerting. I suggest you change the drive letter here. But if you don't, you can easily change it later.

7. Once you get the options set the way you want them, press the Enter key to create the new compressed drive. It won't take long to create the new drive because Dblspace won't have to compress any data. You should be back in business within a minute or so.

COMPRESSING AN EXISTING DRIVE

When you install DoubleSpace using Express Setup, DoubleSpace compresses the data on your first hard disk partition, drive C. If you have additional hard disk partitions or logical drives, you can use the Compress menu's Existing Drive command to compress those partitions and drives as well. You can use this command only once per drive; to create additional compressed drives on a drive you've already compressed, you use the Create New Drive command instead. (Be sure you've logged on to your network too.)

Here's the procedure for compressing an additional hard disk partition or drive that already contains data:

1. Start the Dblspace program by typing *dblspace* at the MS-DOS command prompt. Then from the Compress menu choose the Existing Drive command. Dblspace will display a list of drives you haven't compressed yet, as in the example shown in Figure 6-6.

   For each eligible drive, Dblspace lists the current amount of free space and an estimate of how much free space will exist on the drive after it's compressed.

2. Choose the drive you want to compress by highlighting it and pressing the Enter key. Dblspace then prompts you for the amount of free space to leave on the host if you want to change the default and for the drive letter to assign to the new host if you want to change that default, as in the example shown in Figure 6-7.

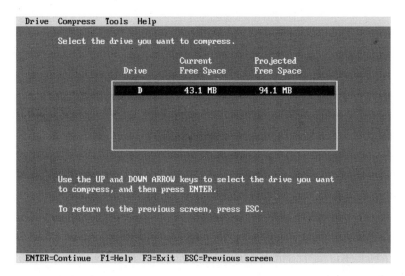

Figure 6-6. *The Existing Drive command's display of eligible—that is, existing uncompressed—drives.*

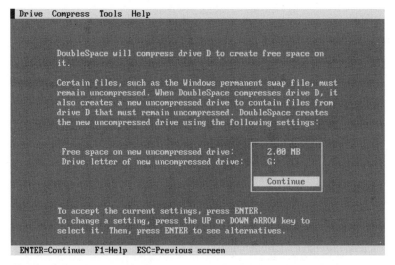

Figure 6-7. *The Existing Drive command's display of the default free space setting for the new host drive and the default drive letter settings, offering you a chance to change the settings.*

If you want to, you can change the amount of free space to leave on the host drive. Dblspace will use a default compression ratio of 2.0 to 1 to calculate the free space on the compressed drive, so every 1MB of free space you leave on the host will reduce the free space on the compressed drive by 2MB. If you want to change the drive letter Dblspace will assign to the host for this compressed drive, now's the time to change it. There's little reason to, though, unless the drive letter selected by Dblspace conflicts with the letter for a network drive, removable hard disk, CD-ROM, or some other type of device that requires a drive letter.

3. When you get the options set the way you want them, press the Enter key to compress the drive. As when you first installed DoubleSpace, the data compression takes about a minute per megabyte, so be sure to allow plenty of time.

DoubleSpacing a RAM Drive

If you've used the RAMDRIVE.SYS device driver to create a RAM drive, you can use DoubleSpace to double the RAM drive's capacity. The procedure is a little tricky. Follow these steps:

1. To create the RAM drive, add a command similar to this one to your CONFIG.SYS file:

```
devicehigh=c:\dos\ramdrive.sys 1160 /e
```

The RAM drive you create must be at least 1.1MB.

2. Restart your computer to activate the RAM drive. Note the drive letter RAMDRIVE.SYS assigns to the RAM drive—in this example, drive D.

3. Use the Dblspace /compress command to compress the RAM drive:

```
dblspace /compress d: /reserve=0
```

4. Use the Dblspace /list command to determine the host drive for the compressed RAM drive—in this example, the host drive is drive G.

CHANGING DOUBLESPACE
DRIVE ASSIGNMENTS

The sequence in which DoubleSpace assigns drive letters to compressed drives and host drives often leaves you with gaps in your drive assignments. For example, you might wind up with a compressed C drive and a compressed G drive on an H host drive but no D, E, or F drive. Most users find these gaps confusing, but the drive assignments are easy enough to change. To change the drive letter assigned to a compressed drive, you use the command-line Dblspace /unmount and /mount commands. To change the drive letter assigned to a host drive, you use the command-line

5. Remove the attributes of the compressed RAM drive's CVF:

```
attrib g:\dblspace.000 -s -h -r
```

6. Copy the compressed RAM drive's CVF to a directory on your C drive.

```
copy g:\dblspace.000 c:\ramdrive
```

7. Now, add the following commands to your AUTOEXEC.BAT file:

```
copy c:\ramdrive\dblspace.000 d:
attrib d:\dblspace.000 +s +h +r
dblspace /mount d: /new=g
```

These lines copy the CVF to the RAM drive, reset its attributes, and mount it. The exact location of these lines in your AUTO-EXEC.BAT file doesn't matter, as long as they're together.

Remember that any files you put on a RAM drive are lost when you restart your computer or turn it off. If you want to save files you've created on a RAM drive, just copy the DBLSPACE.000 file from the host drive back to your C drive before you shut down your computer.

Dblspace /host command in MS-DOS 6.2. In MS-DOS 6.0, the only way to change the hard drive letter assignment is to directly edit the DBLSPACE.INI file, which keeps track of the drive assignments.

Warning: Before you change DoubleSpace-assigned drive letters, realize that you might have to reconfigure applications that expect to find files by means of the old drive letter assignments.

Changing a Compressed Drive Letter

If you don't like the drive letter DoubleSpace assigned to one of your compressed drives, you can change the letter from the command line using two variants of the Dblspace command. (Unfortunately, you can't make the change from Dblspace program menu commands. You'll have to hunker down and use the command line.)

1. Make a note of the compressed drive's CVF file name and host drive letter. Use the Dblspace /list command to display the file name and host drive letter.

2. Now, use the Dblspace /unmount command to *unmount* the compressed drive whose letter you want to change:

   ```
   C:\> dblspace /unmount g:
   ```

   The Dblspace /unmount command will make compressed drive G temporarily unavailable. The compressed drive's CVF still exists, but DoubleSpace disables access to it.

3. Next, use the Dblspace /mount command to reactivate the CVF, this time using a different letter for its compressed drive:

   ```
   C:\> dblspace /mount=001 h: /new=d:
   ```

   This command is a little tricky, so let's look at it piece by piece:

   - */mount=001* tells Dblspace to mount the CVF whose extension is 001—in other words, DBLSPACE.001. You'll have checked the Dblspace /list output in step 1 to find the correct CVF file name extension.

   - *h:* is the host drive that contains the CVF for the compressed drive you want to mount. Again, you'll have checked the Dblspace /list output in step 1 to find the host drive letter.

- */new=d:* makes D the drive letter you want Dblspace to assign to the old compressed drive. The compressed drive is remounted as drive D.

4. Finally, run Dblspace /list again to see if the compressed drive letter reassignment worked.

Changing a Host Drive Letter

Remounting the compressed drive is a good way to change drive assignments when you don't like the letter DoubleSpace has assigned to a compressed drive. But Dblspace /unmount and /mount won't help you if you want to change the letter DoubleSpace has assigned to a host drive. The procedure for doing that depends on whether you're using MS-DOS 6.0 or 6.2. It's a heck of a lot easier if you have 6.2.

Changing the Host Drive Letter in MS-DOS 6.2

To change the letter assigned to a host drive in MS-DOS 6.2, you use the Dblspace command with the /host switch, this way:

```
C:\> dblspace c: /host=e:
```

Here, the letter used for the host of compressed drive C is changed to E. The change doesn't actually take effect until you reboot your computer.

Changing the Host Drive Letter in MS-DOS 6.0

Unfortunately, the MS-DOS 6.0 Dblspace command doesn't accommodate the /host switch. To change the host drive letter in MS-DOS 6.0, you have to roll up your sleeves and edit the DBLSPACE.INI file, which contains the DoubleSpace drive assignments along with other critical information.

Warning: Before we look at how to edit the DBLSPACE.INI file, beware! Editing DBLSPACE.INI is not for the faint of heart. DBLSPACE.INI is a critical file, and the parameters you're going to change can be confusing. If you mess up, DoubleSpace won't be able to access your compressed files unless you have a backup copy of DBLSPACE.INI. Be careful! Make a backup copy of DBLSPACE.INI first.

1. DBLSPACE.INI is a system, hidden, and read-only file in the root directory of drive C's host drive. You'll have to change the file's attributes before you can edit it. Switch to your host drive and enter the command to change the file attributes:

```
H:\> attrib -s -h -r dblspace.ini
```

2. Then, make a backup copy of DBLSPACE.INI, just in case something goes wrong:

```
H:\> copy dblspace.ini dblspace.bak
```

3. Edit DBLSPACE.INI with the MS-DOS Edit command:

```
H:\> edit dblspace.ini
```

Or use your favorite editor.

4. Your DBLSPACE.INI file should look something like this:

```
MaxRemovableDrives=2
FirstDrive=D
LastDrive=J
MaxFileFragments=130
ActivateDrive=H,C0
```

Suppose you want to change the host drive letter from H to E. The line that will assign the host drive letter is the last one: *ActivateDrive=H,C0*. *ActivateDrive* is roughly equivalent to the Dblspace /mount command: when you boot your computer, DoubleSpace mounts the compressed drives according to the DBLSPACE.INI *ActivateDrive* settings.

To change the host drive letter from H to E, all you have to do is edit that last line so that it looks like this:

```
ActivateDrive=E,C0
```

5. Save the file, and restore it to its system, hidden, and read-only status with this command:

```
H:\> attrib +s +h +r dblspace.ini
```

6. Reboot your computer. If something's gone wrong, replace the messed-up version of DBLSPACE.INI with the backup copy you wisely made before you started, and reboot again.

I hope you're sufficiently daunted by this discussion of editing DBLSPACE.INI to be reluctant to fool with it unless you really need to. Be careful when you do.

SUMMARY

DoubleSpace is flexible enough that you can create just about any type of configuration of compressed and host drives you can imagine. Most of us will want to keep it simple.

■ Use the Dblspace Compress menu's Create New Drive command to create a second or third compressed drive on an existing host drive.

■ Use the Dblspace Compress menu's Existing Drive command when you have additional disk partitions you want to compress.

■ If your hard disk has more than one partition, consider combining the partitions into a single primary partition and using multiple compressed volumes instead.

■ To change the drive letter assigned to a compressed volume, unmount it and then remount it using the Dblspace /unmount and /mount commands.

■ To change the drive letter assigned to a host drive, use the Dblspace /host command (MS-DOS 6.2) or edit the DBLSPACE.INI file (MS-DOS 6.0)—but edit DBLSPACE.INI only if you've got chutzpah.

Not that it's easy, mind you.

—Tigger, *The House at Pooh Corner*

Chapter 7

Working with Compressed Floppies and Removable Drives

DoubleSpace isn't just for your hard disk. Once you've installed DoubleSpace on your hard disk, you can use the Dblspace program to double the capacity of your floppy disks too. If your computer has a 1.44MB floppy disk drive, you can store 2.88MB or more of data on its floppy disks.

As you'll see, the MS-DOS 6.0 version of DoubleSpace was handicapped by an inability to automatically recognize floppy disks that had been compressed. If you're using DoubleSpace in MS-DOS 6.0, you must issue a command at the MS-DOS command prompt to access a compressed floppy disk. MS-DOS 6.2 overcomes this limitation. You can set up the MS-DOS 6.2 version of DoubleSpace so that it automatically recognizes a compressed floppy disk when you insert it in the drive. You won't have to issue an MS-DOS command to access the compressed floppy disk.

DoubleSpace can also be used with removable hard drives, such as those made by Bernoulli and SyQuest. Using DoubleSpace with a removable hard drive is similar to using it with a floppy disk. We'll look at using DoubleSpace with both floppy disks and removable drives.

COMPRESSING A FLOPPY DISK

When you use the Dblspace program to compress a floppy disk, Dblspace creates a Compressed Volume File (CVF) on the disk and compresses all of the data on the disk, moving it into the CVF as it compresses it. As with a hard disk's CVF, DoubleSpace mounts a floppy disk's CVF using the floppy drive's original drive letter. It also assigns a drive letter to the uncompressed host drive. You can't create more than one CVF on a floppy disk as you can on a hard disk, though.

Before you compress a floppy disk, note the following:

- The floppy disk must be formatted. DoubleSpace can't compress an unformatted disk.

- The floppy disk can be empty or it can contain data. However, there must be at least 650KB (513KB in MS-DOS 6.2) of free space on the disk. DoubleSpace can't compress a full disk.

- You can't compress a 360KB disk. That makes sense when you think about it. A 360KB disk can't possibly meet the requirement that the disk to be compressed have at least 650KB (513KB in MS-DOS 6.2) of free space.

You can compress a floppy disk using either the Compress menu's Existing Drive command or the compress command-line switch.

Compressing a Floppy Disk from the Menu

To compress a floppy disk using the Compress menu's Existing Drive command:

1. Insert a formatted disk in the floppy drive. The disk can contain data or it can be empty, but it must contain at least 650KB (513KB in MS-DOS 6.2) of free space.

2. Start up the Dblspace program by typing *dblspace* at the MS-DOS command prompt.

3. From the Compress menu, choose the Existing Drive command. (You can't use the Compress menu's Create New Drive command with floppy disks.) Dblspace will search all of your disk drives, including floppy drives, for disks that can be compressed. Then it will display a screen similar to the one in Figure 7-1 on the next page.

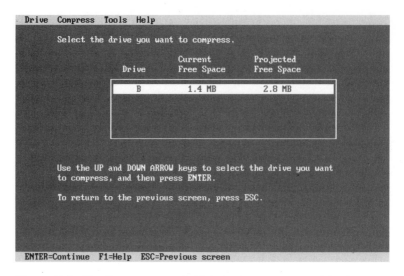

Figure 7-1. *The Compress menu's Existing Drive command displaying a list of eligible drives—that is, existing uncompressed drives with at least 650KB (513KB in MS-DOS 6.2) of free space.*

4. If more than one uncompressed drive appears in the list, use the arrow keys to highlight the one you want to compress and then press the Enter key.

5. When Dblspace displays its confirmation screen, press C to compress the disk.

It doesn't take long to compress a floppy. If the disk contains data, it might take a few minutes. If the disk is empty or nearly empty, it should take only a few moments. (If you're using MS-DOS 6.2, it takes a little longer because ScanDisk performs a surface analysis.)

Compressing a Floppy Disk from the Command Line

To compress a floppy disk from the command line:

- Enter the Dblspace /compress command:

```
C:\> dblspace /compress a:
```

This command compresses the floppy disk in drive A.

- To compress a disk in drive B, type *dblspace /compress b:* instead.

A Batch File to Compress a Floppy

If you frequently compress floppy disks, you might want to create a simple batch file that contains a Dblspace /compress command. The COMPRESS.BAT batch file contains not only a Dblspace /compress command but also commands that check to make sure the drive isn't already compressed.

```
@echo off
if "%1"=="" goto Error1
if exist %1\readthis.txt goto Error2
dblspace /compress %1
goto End
:Error1
echo You must specify a drive letter.
goto End
:Error2
echo The disk in drive %1 is already compressed.
:End
```

To use COMPRESS.BAT, insert a formatted floppy disk in the drive (drive A here) and type

```
compress a:
```

USING A COMPRESSED FLOPPY WITH MS-DOS 6.0

Note: Microsoft significantly improved DoubleSpace's handling of compressed floppy disks with MS-DOS 6.2 by enabling you to configure DoubleSpace so that it automatically recognizes and mounts compressed floppy drives. This feature is described later in this chapter.

Using a compressed floppy disk with MS-DOS 6.0 is a little more complicated than using a compressed hard disk. DoubleSpace automatically mounts compressed hard drives whenever you start up your computer, so the compressed drive is always available. In MS-DOS 6.0, a compressed floppy disk is not automatically mounted. After you compress a floppy disk, DoubleSpace unmounts it if you remove the disk from the drive and access another disk in that drive or if you shut down your computer. Before you can access the compressed floppy disk again, you must use a Dblspace /mount command to mount it.

Keep these points in mind as you work with a compressed floppy disk using MS-DOS 6.0:

- When you first compress a floppy disk, DoubleSpace automatically mounts it. There's no need to use the Dblspace /mount command immediately after compressing a floppy.

- Although Dblspace provides an Unmount command on its Drive menu and an /unmount command-line switch, there's little reason to unmount a compressed floppy disk in MS-DOS 6.0. DoubleSpace automatically unmounts a compressed floppy when you remove it from the drive and access another disk in that drive or when you restart your computer.

- If you mount a compressed floppy and then replace it with another compressed floppy, you must mount the new floppy separately in MS-DOS 6.0.

- You can't run DoubleSpace commands from within *Microsoft Windows*. If you're running MS-DOS 6.0, to mount a compressed floppy you must exit *Windows,* run DoubleSpace /mount, and then restart *Windows*. And you have to do that every time you replace one compressed floppy with another. If you're a *Windows* and MS-DOS 6.0 user and had visions of doubling the capacity of all your floppy disks, you'd better think again. Not being able to mount a compressed floppy from *Windows* is enough of an inconvenience to make compressed floppies more trouble than they're worth for *Windows* users. Better upgrade to MS-DOS 6.2.

The READTHIS.TXT File

When DoubleSpace compresses a floppy disk, it adds a file named READTHIS.TXT to the root directory of the uncompressed host. As a result, if you list the directory of an unmounted compressed disk, this is what you'll see:

```
Volume in drive B is HOST_FOR_B
Directory of B:\

READTHIS TXT      350 09-30-93   8:28a
     1 file(s)      350 bytes
            459776 bytes free
```

The size of the 6.2 version of READTHIS.TXT is different. Here are the contents of this file. As you can see, it contains the instructions for mounting the compressed disk. (The 6.2 version is similar.)

```
This disk has been compressed by MS-DOS 6 DoubleSpace.

To make this disk's contents accessible, change to the drive that contains it,
and then type the following at the command prompt:

  DBLSPACE/MOUNT

(If this file is located on a drive other than the drive that contains the
compressed disk, then the disk has already been mounted.)
```

Mounting a Compressed Floppy from the Command Line (MS-DOS 6.0)

The instructions in the READTHIS.TXT file say to change to the drive that contains the floppy disk and type *dblspace /mount*. It's easier, though, to specify the drive letter in the Dblspace /mount command, this way:

```
C:\> dblspace /mount a:
```

This command mounts the compressed floppy in drive A. Once the floppy is mounted, you can access its data as if it were any other floppy disk. The only difference is that the floppy now has increased capacity.

When you mount a compressed floppy, DoubleSpace reassigns a drive letter to the host drive for the compressed floppy, just as it does for a compressed hard drive. You don't need to worry about this drive letter, since the host drive for a compressed floppy rarely has files on it (other than the CVF and the READTHIS.TXT file, of course).

Mounting a Compressed Floppy from the Drive Menu (MS-DOS 6.0)

You can also mount a compressed floppy from Dblspace using the Drive menu's Mount command.

1. Insert the disk you want to mount in the drive.

2. From the Drive menu, choose the Mount command. Dblspace lists all of the unmounted compressed drives that are currently available.

Usually, there will be only one, as in the example shown in Figure 7-2.

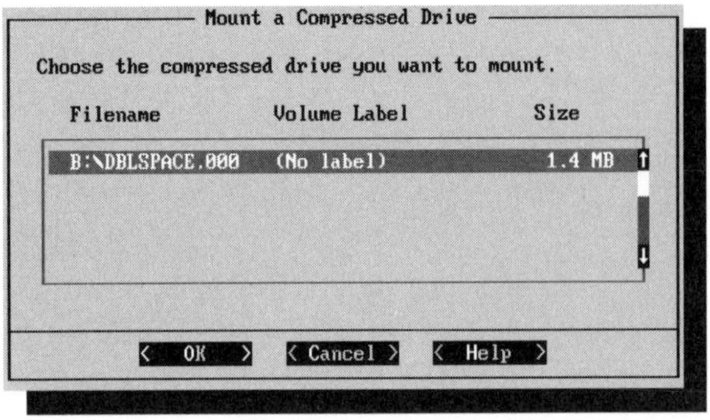

```
┌──────────────── Mount a Compressed Drive ────────────────┐
│                                                           │
│  Choose the compressed drive you want to mount.           │
│                                                           │
│     Filename          Volume Label          Size          │
│  ┌──────────────────────────────────────────────────┐    │
│  │ B:\DBLSPACE.000   (No label)            1.4 MB  ↑ │    │
│  │                                                   │    │
│  │                                                   │    │
│  │                                                 ↓ │    │
│  └──────────────────────────────────────────────────┘    │
│                                                           │
│        〈   OK   〉    〈 Cancel 〉    〈  Help  〉          │
└───────────────────────────────────────────────────────────┘
```

Figure 7-2. *Mounting a compressed drive from the Drive menu.*

3. Use the arrow keys to highlight the drive containing the disk you want to mount, and then press the Enter key.

USING A COMPRESSED FLOPPY WITH MS-DOS 6.2

With MS-DOS 6.2, Microsoft improved DoubleSpace's support for compressed floppy disks by providing a facility to automatically recognize and mount them. You no longer have to use the Dblspace /mount command to access a compressed floppy. This is especially good news for *Microsoft Windows* users since you can't issue the Dblspace /mount command during a *Windows* session.

The Automount feature is enabled by default, but you can disable it by using the Options command available from the Dblspace Tools menu or by using the Dblspace /automount command. Why would you want to disable the Automount feature? Because it adds about 4KB to DoubleSpace's memory requirements. If you don't use compressed floppies much, you can free up that 4KB by disabling Automount.

To disable Automount from the command line, use this command:

```
C:\> dblspace /automount=0
```

This command adds a line to the DBLSPACE.INI file that disables the Automount feature. Automount won't actually be disabled until you restart your computer.

If you've disabled Automount and want to enable it again, use this command at the MS-DOS prompt:

```
C:\> dblspace /automount=1
```

Again, the change won't be effective until you reboot.

You can also enable Automount for only specific drives. You might want to do that if you have a removable hard disk for which you want the Automount feature to be enabled but you don't want it to be enabled for your floppy disks. To enable Automount for a specific drive, specify the drive letter:

```
C:\> dblspace /automount=D
```

Now, Automount will be enabled only for drive D. (Note that in order to enable Automount for specific drives, you must use the Dblspace /automount switch. The Options command on the Dblspace Tools menu lets you enable or disable Automount, but not for specific drives.)

USING DOUBLESPACE WITH A REMOVABLE HARD DRIVE

Removable hard drives, such as those made by Bernoulli or SyQuest, have become increasingly popular among users who need lots of disk storage. A removable hard drive is similar to a floppy drive: the medium (that is, the disk itself) is housed in a cartridge that can be removed from the drive. Typically, the capacity of each cartridge is 40MB or 80MB. With DoubleSpace, you can double the capacity of each cartridge. Because the cost of removable disk cartridges is high, DoubleSpace is especially beneficial when you use a removable drive.

Most removable drives require that you add a device driver to your CONFIG.SYS file. This device driver monitors the removable drive so that it knows when you've removed a disk and inserted another. With MS-DOS 6.0, DoubleSpace has no such capability, though, so you need to manually mount a compressed removable disk when you insert it. If your removable drive were drive E, you would use this command to mount a compressed removable disk:

```
C:\> dblspace /mount e:
```

Consider adding a Dblspace /mount command to your AUTOEXEC.BAT file. Because the removable drive's device driver is required if MS-DOS is to recognize the drive, DoubleSpace can't mount the drive automatically. DoubleSpace mounts compressed drives *before* MS-DOS processes the CONFIG.SYS file. As a result, when DoubleSpace is mounting your compressed drives, the driver that's required to support the removable drive hasn't been loaded yet. So the removable drive isn't mounted unless you explicitly mount it or have your AUTOEXEC.BAT file mount it for you.

Note that with MS-DOS 6.2, the Automount feature can automatically mount removable hard drives. So the Dblspace /mount command isn't necessary.

SUMMARY

DoubleSpace lets you compress floppy disks and removable disk drives. MS-DOS 6.0 doesn't automatically mount them, which limits the usefulness of compressed floppy drives, especially for *Windows* users. Fortunately, MS-DOS 6.2 does automatically mount compressed floppy disks and removable drives. Given the amount of data a compressed removable drive can store and the cost of removable disk cartridges, it makes sense to compress removable drives.

- To compress a floppy disk, use the Compress menu's Existing Drive command or the Dblspace /compress command.

- To mount a compressed floppy, use the Drive menu's Mount command or the Dblspace /mount command.

- To unmount a compressed floppy, remove it from the drive and access another disk in that drive or shut down your computer, or use the Drive menu's Unmount command or the Dblspace /unmount command.

- Compressed removable drives are similar to compressed floppies. It's a good idea to add a Dblspace /mount command to your AUTOEXEC.BAT file.

Bother

—Winnie the Pooh

Chapter 8

DoubleSpace Troubleshooting

DoubleSpace is one of the most thoroughly tested computer programs ever released. But with the number of MS-DOS 6.0 and 6.2 users already in the millions, some DoubleSpace users are bound to run into problems. Let's hope you're not one of them. If you're not so lucky, this chapter should help you out. It addresses the most common problems encountered by DoubleSpace users.

Of course, the best way to deal with DoubleSpace problems is to avoid them altogether. In a way, this entire book is about avoiding DoubleSpace problems. If you understand what DoubleSpace is and how it works, you're well on your way to avoiding DoubleSpace trouble. And if you take the precautions recommended in Chapter 3 before you install DoubleSpace, you probably won't even bother to read this chapter.

We'll start out by looking at some general troubleshooting procedures. Then, we'll look at 16 common DoubleSpace problems. To create some sense of order, I've categorized the 16 problems into four groups: startup problems, problems turned up by ScanDisk (MS-DOS 6.2) and Chkdsk that relate to a damaged Compressed Volume File (CVF), problems related to disk space and excessive fragmentation, and problems related to using DoubleSpace with *Microsoft Windows*.

GENERAL TROUBLESHOOTING PROCEDURES

If you encounter a problem with DoubleSpace, it's helpful to be acquainted with a few basic troubleshooting procedures. Not all of the procedures apply to every situation, of course.

Booting Clean

Because software comes in a nearly infinite variety of configurations, DoubleSpace can occasionally run into a software incompatibility. When that happens, it's a good idea to boot your system clean, with no memory resident software that might cause a conflict. If DoubleSpace runs fine when you boot clean, you can reintroduce memory resident programs one at a time until you find the one that causes the problem.

Before MS-DOS 6, booting clean was a hassle. But MS-DOS 6.0 and 6.2 provide two simple techniques for booting clean:

■ To completely bypass your CONFIG.SYS and AUTOEXEC.BAT files, which might load some offending memory resident programs, restart your computer. When you see the message *Starting MS-DOS,* press and then release the F5 key, or press and hold the shift key.

■ To selectively process lines in your CONFIG.SYS file, press and then release F8 instead of F5. Then, MS-DOS will prompt you for each line of your CONFIG.SYS file, as in this prompt:

```
DEVICE=C:\DOS\HIMEM.SYS [Y,N]?
```

You can press Y to process the line or N to ignore it. Use this selective processing feature to reintroduce memory resident programs, starting with the ones that load MS-DOS into high memory and activate upper memory.

If you're using MS-DOS 6.2, the F8 key selectively processes the lines in your AUTOEXEC.BAT file as well.

Note: Using the F5 and F8 keys to boot clean doesn't help solve software conflicts that prevent DoubleSpace from completing its setup routine. That's because DoubleSpace Setup reboots your computer midway through its process, causing your CONFIG.SYS and AUTOEXEC.BAT files to be executed once again. If you're having trouble installing DoubleSpace and you believe an errant memory resident program might be at fault, edit your CONFIG.SYS and AUTOEXEC.BAT files to temporarily comment out (put a REM command in front of) commands that start up the suspect memory resident program.

Disabling DoubleSpace

When you boot clean by pressing F5, MS-DOS bypasses your CONFIG.SYS and AUTOEXEC.BAT files but still activates Double-Space. If DoubleSpace hangs when it tries to mount your compressed C drive, you'll have to boot without activating DoubleSpace. That's easy to do with MS-DOS 6.2: just press the Ctrl+F5 combination when the message *Starting MS-DOS* appears.

With MS-DOS 6.0, you must boot from a drive that doesn't have the system file DBLSPACE.BIN if you want to start up without activating DoubleSpace. The easiest way to do that is to boot from a floppy disk that doesn't contain DBLSPACE.BIN. If you created a DoubleSpace panic disk when you installed DoubleSpace, you can temporarily rename its DBLSPACE.BIN file using this sequence of commands:

```
A:\> attrib dblspace.bin -s -h -r
A:\> rename dblspace.bin dblspace.sav
```

Using EMM386.EXE Safely

EMM386.EXE is the MS-DOS expanded memory manager. It scans upper memory to determine which areas it can use to create Upper Memory Blocks, into which MS-DOS can load memory resident programs or device drivers. You activate EMM386.EXE by including a *Device=c:\dos\emm386.exe* command in the CONFIG.SYS file.

The MS-DOS 6.0 and 6.2 versions of EMM386.EXE have a new switch, Highscan, which searches upper memory more aggressively. In some cases, the Highscan switch causes EMM386.EXE to use an upper memory area that it shouldn't, which results in a memory conflict that can cause your system to lock up.

Although the Highscan switch has nothing to do with DoubleSpace, DoubleSpace has often been blamed for problems that are actually caused by Highscan. That's why I mention it here.

Then, reboot your computer. To restore the file to its rightful name, use this sequence of commands:

```
A:\> rename dblspace.sav dblspace.bin
A:\> attrib dblspace.bin +s +h +r
```

Enabling DoubleGuard (MS-DOS 6.2 Only)

MS-DOS 6.2 includes a feature called DoubleGuard, which helps protect DoubleSpace from software conflicts that corrupt the contents of memory used by DoubleSpace. DoubleGuard works by monitoring DoubleSpace's memory, performing frequent checksum checks to see whether buffer data has been inadvertently modified. (A checksum test is a common technique for quickly verifying that the contents of memory has not changed.) If a checksum error occurs, the most likely cause is that a misbehaving program has overwritten DoubleSpace's memory.

When you install DoubleSpace, the DoubleGuard feature is automatically enabled. I recommend that you leave DoubleGuard on indefinitely; the increased safety is worth the slight performance penalty imposed by DoubleGuard. Because disabling DoubleGuard does speed up your computer, some users disable DoubleGuard if it doesn't report any errors after a week or so of use. You can disable DoubleGuard using the Dblspace /doublguard command:

```
C:\> dblspace /doublguard=0
```

Restart your computer so that the changes will take effect.

If you do disable DoubleGuard, though, you should reactivate it before you install new software. You can enable DoubleGuard using the Dblspace /doublguard command:

```
C:\> dblspace /doublguard=1
```

Restart your computer so that the changes will take effect. Then, install the new software and let DoubleGuard run for a week or so to see whether any errors pop up. If DoubleGuard doesn't report any errors, you can probably safely disable DoubleGuard again.

You can also enable or disable DoubleGuard by typing *dblspace* at the command prompt and choosing the Options command from the DoubleSpace Tools menu.

Defragmenting a Compressed Drive

Because DoubleSpace allocates disk space by sector rather than by cluster, a compressed drive is more prone to fragmentation than an uncompressed drive. Because a disproportionate number of problems are caused by excessive fragmentation in a compressed drive, defragmenting a compressed drive is a common DoubleSpace troubleshooting procedure.

The MS-DOS 6.0 and 6.2 Defrag command can defragment a Double-Space drive, but if you've encountered problems from fragmentation, you might need to use a more thorough procedure. To thoroughly defragment a compressed drive, run these two commands in succession:

```
dblspace /defrag /f
```

and

```
defrag
```

These commands might take several hours to complete execution, so you might want to combine them into a batch file and run them overnight.

Delete-tracking programs such as *Mirror* (which comes with both MS-DOS 5 and *PC Tools*) and *Image* (which comes with *The Norton Utilities*) can prevent DoubleSpace from completely defragmenting a DoubleSpace drive that was created by compressing an existing hard disk. That's because they create an unformatting file at the end of the drive. Such programs assign the system and hidden attributes to the unformatting file, so Defrag can't move the file as it defragments the drive. For more information about how to remove an unformatting file from your disk or how to change its attributes so that Defrag can move it, see the section "Defrag doesn't fully defragment a drive" and the sidebar "Why Is *Mirror* So Troublesome?" later in this chapter.

In the meantime, make sure your AUTOEXEC.BAT file doesn't contain a *Mirror* or an *Image* command.

Scanning the Disk Surface

Because DoubleSpace uses the sectors on your disk more efficiently than the sectors would otherwise be used, it's more likely to discover defects in your disk drive's recording surfaces. These defects aren't caused by DoubleSpace. They might have been on the disk originally, or they might have developed over time. They can lie dormant for months, only to turn up shortly after you install DoubleSpace. Naturally, DoubleSpace gets the blame.

To detect and lock out disk surface defects, you should periodically run a surface analysis program such as the MS-DOS 6.2 *ScanDisk* program, *Calibrate* or *NDD* from *The Norton Utilities*, or *Diskfix* from *PC Tools*. If you're using MS-DOS 6.0, you should run one of these utilities before you install DoubleSpace. MS-DOS 6.2 automatically runs ScanDisk when you install DoubleSpace, so this step isn't necessary. After you've installed DoubleSpace, you should perform a surface analysis periodically—once every three months or so. You'll also want to run a surface analysis program whenever you encounter a problem that might have been caused by a surface defect.

Resizing a Compressed Drive (MS-DOS 6.0 Only)

If you're using MS-DOS 6.0, you can sometimes solve elusive DoubleSpace problems simply by resizing a compressed drive. (In MS-DOS 6.2, you can deal better with such problems by running ScanDisk.) Here's the procedure:

1. Type *dblspace /list*. Note the amount of free space on the host drive for the compressed drive.

2. Type *dblspace /size*. The /size switch resizes the drive, leaving as much free space on the host drive as possible. There will be almost no free space on the compressed drive.

3. Type *dblspace /size /reserve =n*, where *n* is the amount of free space in megabytes that was originally present on the host drive. For example, if you originally had 2MB of free space on the host, use this command:

```
C:\> dblspace /size /reserve=2.
```

This restores the free space that was present in the compressed drive.

Changing DBLSPACE.INI Settings

The solutions to several of the problems described in this chapter require that you change one or more settings in the file DBLSPACE.INI, a system, hidden, read-only file in the root directory of your host drive.

With MS-DOS 6.2, Microsoft added several switches to the Dblspace command that let you change settings in DBLSPACE.INI without directly editing the file. For example, to change the *MaxFileFragments* setting, you can use a command like this one:

```
C:\> dblspace /maxfilefragments=200
```

If you're using MS-DOS 6.0, you must directly edit the DBLSPACE.INI file to change its settings. To do that, you must first change the file's attributes, using the Attrib command:

```
H:\> attrib dblspace.ini -s -h -r
```

When you've finished editing DBLSPACE.INI, reset the attributes:

```
H:\> attrib dblspace.ini +s +h +r
```

Be aware that the contents of DBLSPACE.INI are critical. If you mess this file up, DoubleSpace might not run properly. Always make a backup copy of DBLSPACE.INI before you edit it, and carefully follow instructions for editing the file for a given situation. If you have occasion to edit DBLSPACE.INI, it wouldn't be a bad idea to look ahead to Chapter 13, where the purpose of each line in DBLSPACE.INI is described. Or better yet, upgrade to MS-DOS 6.2 so that you won't have to edit the file directly.

16 COMMON DOUBLESPACE PROBLEMS

The most common DoubleSpace problems and some suggestions, grouped roughly into four categories, follow.

Startup Problems

Many DoubleSpace problems show up right away, when you start up your computer.

You receive the message *A CVF is damaged* when you start up your computer. This ominous message is not nearly so bad as it sounds. When you start your computer, DoubleSpace automatically mounts your compressed hard drives. And when it mounts a compressed hard drive, DoubleSpace automatically performs the equivalent of a Chkdsk command, checking the CVF's internal structures for errors. If DoubleSpace finds any errors, it displays the message *A CVF is damaged.*

If you receive this message and you're using MS-DOS 6.2, run the ScanDisk command to correct the problem. If you're using MS-DOS 6.0, run the Chkdsk /f command. Turn to the section "ScanDisk and CVF Problems," later in the chapter, for information about error messages displayed by ScanDisk and Chkdsk.

You receive the message *Too many block devices* when you start your computer. MS-DOS can support as many as 26 logical drives, using the letters A through Z. The message *Too many block devices* is displayed when you try to set up more than 26 logical drives.

When DoubleSpace starts up, it reserves for itself all drive letters between the last physical drive (usually C) and the drive letter specified in the DBLSPACE.INI file's *LastDrive* line. If you create additional drives by installing a device driver such as RAMDRIVE.SYS or the driver used by a removable hard drive or by a CD-ROM drive, DoubleSpace still holds on to the number of drives it reserved when it started. In extreme cases, this can push the total number of drives beyond the limit of 26.

The most likely cause of the *Too many block devices* problem is that you reserved too many drives in the *LastDrive* setting. For example, if you set *LastDrive* to Z and then you try to create a RAM drive, you'll exceed the 26-drive limit. To correct this problem, run the Dblspace program, from the Tools menu select the Options command, and change the *LastDrive* setting to reserve fewer drives. Then reboot your computer to make the change effective.

If you're using MS-DOS 6.2, you can change the *LastDrive* setting from the command line using the Dblspace /lastdrive command:

```
C:\> dblspace /lastdrive=h
```

Note that you can't change the *LastDrive* setting to a letter that comes before the letter assigned to the host drive. You can change the host drive letter using the Dblspace /host command:

```
C:\> dblspace c: /host=h
```

This sets the host drive letter for compressed drive C to H. You must reboot before these changes take effect.

If you have MS-DOS 6.0, you must edit the DBLSPACE.INI file to change the *LastDrive* and host drive settings. Here's the procedure:

1. Make the host drive of your compressed C drive the current drive.

2. Remove the attributes of DBLSPACE.INI with this command (assuming the host drive is H):

```
H:\> attrib dblspace.ini -s -h -r
```

3. Start up the MS-DOS Edit command or your favorite editor to edit DBLSPACE.INI.

4. Usually, you should set *LastDrive* to the fifth letter after your last physical drive. For example, if you have one hard drive (drive C), set *LastDrive* to H.

   Suppose DBLSPACE.INI contains this line:

```
LastDrive=Z
```

   To change *LastDrive* to H, edit this line so that it looks like this:

```
LastDrive=H
```

5. The host drive letter you choose must fall within the drive letters reserved for DoubleSpace use by the *LastDrive* line. The host drive letter is assigned by the second parameter of the *ActivateDrive* line. (Note that if the CVF extension number is .000, the host drive letter and the CVF drive letter are swapped after the DoubleSpace drive is mounted.) If you need to, change this line to assign a host drive letter that's within the range reserved by *LastDrive*.

   For example, suppose DBLSPACE.INI contains an *ActivateDrive* line that assigns drive H as the host drive:

```
ActivateDrive=H,C0
```

To change the host drive letter to G, edit the line so that it looks like this one:

```
ActivateDrive=G,C0
```

6. Save the file and exit from your editor.

7. Restore the attributes of DBLSPACE.INI with this command (again assuming that the host drive is H):

```
H:\> attrib dblspace.ini +s +h +r
```

8. Restart your computer so that the changes will take effect.

You can't access a network drive. When you install DoubleSpace, the installation routine works around any drive letters that are already in use. That's why you should log on to your network before you install DoubleSpace. If you find that a network drive is not accessible after you've installed DoubleSpace, it's probably because DoubleSpace and your networking software are contending for the same drive letter.

This one nailed me the first time I installed DoubleSpace. I was using a LANtastic network and forgot to log on to the network before I installed DoubleSpace. My STARTNET.BAT file (the batch file you run to access a LANtastic network) contained this line:

```
net use h: \\server-1\c-drive
```

This command tried to access the C drive on the server named SERVER-1, assigning it to drive H. Of course, it didn't work because DoubleSpace had already grabbed the letter H for my compressed drive's host drive.

To solve such a problem, you have to change the drive letter used by the host drive or the drive letter used by the network. That's easy to do if you have MS-DOS 6.2; you use the Dblspace /host command:

```
C:\> dblspace c: /host=j
```

Note that you can't change the host drive letter to a letter that's beyond the last drive reserved for DoubleSpace use by the *LastDrive* setting. You can change the *LastDrive* setting by using the Dblspace /lastdrive command:

```
C:\> dblspace /lastdrive=j
```

If you have MS-DOS 6.0, you must edit the DBLSPACE.INI file in order to change the host drive letter. Here's the procedure:

1. Make the host drive the current drive.

2. Remove the attributes of DBLSPACE.INI with this command (assuming the host drive is H):

```
H:\> attrib dblspace.ini -s -h -r
```

3. Start up the MS-DOS Edit command or your favorite editor to edit DBLSPACE.INI.

4. Change the first parameter of the *ActivateDrive* line to the new host drive letter. For example, suppose DBLSPACE.INI contains this line:

```
ActivateDrive=H,C0
```

To change the host drive letter to J, edit this line so it looks like this one:

```
ActivateDrive=J,C0
```

5. The host drive letter you pick must fall within the drive letters reserved for DoubleSpace use by the *LastDrive* line. If you need to, change the *LastDrive* line accordingly.

For example, suppose DBLSPACE.INI contains this line:

```
LastDrive=H
```

To change *LastDrive* to J, edit this line so that it looks like this:

```
LastDrive=J
```

6. Save the file and exit from your editor.

7. Restore the attributes of DBLSPACE.INI with this command (again assuming the host drive is H):

```
H:\> attrib dblspace.ini +s +h +r
```

8. Restart your computer so that the changes will take effect.

The procedure for changing the drive assignments used by your network depend on the network software you're using. Consult your network documentation for more information.

An application program doesn't work after you install Double-Space. If you have an application that worked fine before you installed DoubleSpace but doesn't work after, here are some possible causes and solutions:

- The program is copy protected, and the copy protection scheme doesn't get along with DoubleSpace. You'll have to move the program to an uncompressed drive or reinstall the program from disk, putting it on the uncompressed drive. If that doesn't work, you'll have to contact the software vendor for instructions on how to make the program work with DoubleSpace.

- The program is incompatible with compressed drives. Move the program to an uncompressed drive. It could be that the program's data files are incompatible with compressed drives. In that case, you can move just the data files to an uncompressed drive.

- The program doesn't work because the DoubleSpace system file DBLSPACE.BIN reduced the amount of conventional memory available. If you have an 80386 computer or better, the solution is to make sure DBLSPACE.BIN loads into upper memory by changing the CONFIG.SYS line *Device=c:\dos\dblspace.bin /move* to *Devicehigh=c:\dos\dblspace.bin /move*.

You receive an alert from DoubleGuard (MS-DOS 6.2 only). If DoubleGuard halts your computer with an alert, you probably have an incompatible memory resident program or device driver. DoubleGuard stops your computer cold when it detects a memory conflict, so you'll have to reboot your computer to continue. Here's what to do:

1. Make a note of what you were doing when the alert occurred.

2. Restart your computer.

3. Type *scandisk /all* at the command prompt to detect and correct any errors on your disk drives.

4. See if you can re-create the alert: repeat what you were doing when the alert occurred and see if it happens again.

5. If you suspect that the problem was caused by a memory resident program or device driver, boot clean (press F5 when the message

Starting MS-DOS appears). Then, reintroduce your memory resident programs and device drivers one at a time until the problem recurs.

ScanDisk and CVF Problems

The ScanDisk (MS-DOS 6.2 only) and Chkdsk commands both analyze the directory, FAT, and internal structures of a Compressed Volume File. If any of these structures contains invalid data, ScanDisk and Chkdsk display an appropriate error message.

Note: If you're using MS-DOS 6.2, you should use the ScanDisk command instead of the Chkdsk command. ScanDisk can detect a wider range of DoubleSpace problems than Chkdsk can.

ScanDisk or Chkdsk reports lost allocation units. The most common type of CVF damage is *lost clusters* (aka *lost allocation units*). Lost clusters result from a break in the chain of clusters that belong to a file. The clusters beyond the break in the chain still contain data, but MS-DOS has no way of knowing what file the clusters belong to. It's a phenomenon that resembles that episode of *Star Trek* in which Kirk gets trapped between two universes and is not really a part of either one. Lost clusters don't contain usable data because they're not connected to a file. But because the clusters aren't marked as free space, they can't be allocated to new files. Fascinating.

When ScanDisk detects lost clusters, it asks you whether you want to save or delete them. If you reply Save, ScanDisk creates a file in the root directory for each chain of lost clusters. The first chain of lost clusters will be named FILE0001.CHK, the second FILE0002.CHK, and so on. Once you've converted the lost clusters to files, you can display them with the Type command to see what they contain. Usually, they don't contain any useful information, so you can just delete them. On rare occasions, you'll find the missing part of a text file or some other interesting data. When that happens, you can rename the file and move it to an appropriate directory.

When Chkdsk detects lost clusters, it displays an error message. You must then run the Chkdsk /f command to convert the lost clusters to files.

ScanDisk or Chkdsk reports cross-linked files. Another common problem detected by Chkdsk is *cross-linked files*. This problem occurs when the FAT indicates that a cluster belongs to two or more files. One of the files contains clusters that don't belong to it, and it's possible that both files are jumbled.

Unfortunately, neither ScanDisk nor Chkdsk can fully correct cross-linked files. ScanDisk fixes the cross-linked condition of the FAT by copying the overlapped clusters to each file. However, one or both of the files that were cross-linked will still contain invalid data. You'll have to examine each file to determine whether or not it's damaged. If the file is damaged, delete it and restore a backup copy of the file (a good argument for frequent backups).

The Chkdsk command doesn't do even that much about cross-linked files. If Chkdsk reports cross-linked files, make a note of which files are involved. Then, copy each of the cross-linked files using a new file name and delete the originals. This takes care of the cross-linked condition much as ScanDisk does, but one or both of the files will still contain incorrect data. View each file to determine whether it's damaged. If the file is damaged, delete it and restore a backup copy of the file.

ScanDisk or Chkdsk reports other errors. The ScanDisk and Chkdsk commands might report other problems with the Compressed Volume File besides lost clusters and cross-linked files. When ScanDisk detects an error, it asks you whether you want to fix it. When Chkdsk reports an error, you must run Chkdsk /f to correct the error.

Disk Space and Fragmentation Problems

If you encounter one of the errors described in this section, the most likely cause is that you've run out of disk space or your compressed drive or host drive is suffering from excessive fragmentation.

You run out of space on a compressed drive. If you run out of space on a compressed drive, there could be several causes.

- There might actually be plenty of disk space available for the compressed drive, but the estimated compression ratio might be set too low. Remember that the free space for a compressed drive reported by MS-DOS is just an estimate based on the estimated compression ratio. You can increase the amount of free space reported simply by increasing the compression ratio.

To increase the compression ratio, start Dblspace and use the Drive menu's Change Ratio command. Or type a command similar to this one at the command prompt:

```
C:\> dblspace /ratio=2.5
```

The idea is to set the compression ratio to a value that's as close as possible to the actual compression ratio DoubleSpace will achieve for any new files you put on your compressed drive.

If you can't change the compression ratio, you might need to defragment the drive.

■ If the compressed drive really doesn't have enough disk space, you can increase the size of the Compressed Volume File provided you have free space available on the host drive.

To increase the size of a compressed drive's CVF, start Dblspace and use the Drive menu's Change Size command. Or type a command similar to this one at the command prompt:

```
C:\> dblspace /size /reserve=1.5
```

This command changes the size of the compressed drive's CVF, leaving 1.5MB of free space on the host drive.

If you aren't able to increase the size of the compressed drive's CVF, you might need to free up extra disk space on the host drive by deleting unnecessary files stored uncompressed on the host drive.

■ The compressed drive might be excessively fragmented. When that happens, there might be plenty of available sectors in the compressed drive's CVF, but they might be fragmented so badly that DoubleSpace can't use them for your files. If that's the case, you need to defragment your compressed drive. See "Defragmenting a Compressed Drive" in the "General Troubleshooting Procedures" section at the beginning of this chapter.

You run out of space on the host drive. If your host drive runs out of disk space, you can increase the space available on the host by decreasing the size of your compressed drive's CVF. To do that, start Dblspace and use the Drive menu's Change Size command. Or type a command like this one at the command prompt:

```
C:\> dblspace /size /reserve=3
```

This command changes the size of the CVF for the compressed C drive so that 3MB of free space is available on the host drive.

- If you are unable to reduce the size of the compressed drive, see the next section, "You can't reduce the size of a compressed drive."
- The host drive might be full even though it appears to contain no files. That's because the files on a host drive might be hidden. Use the command Dir /ah to see a listing of the hidden files and their sizes.

You can't reduce the size of a compressed drive. If DoubleSpace displays a message indicating that a compressed drive is too fragmented to resize, you'll have to defragment the drive before you can reduce its size. See "Defragmenting a Compressed Drive" in the "General Troubleshooting Procedures" section at the beginning of this chapter.

Sometimes, DoubleSpace will refuse to reduce the size of a compressed drive because a FAT entry has indicated that a cluster is unreadable. DoubleSpace truncates the FAT when you reduce the size of a CVF, but it won't truncate the FAT below an entry that indicates a cluster is anything other than free. That includes a bad-cluster entry. To get around this problem, use a disk editor such as those found in *The Norton Utilities* or *PC Tools* to change the FAT entry from "Bad" (FFF7) to "Unused" (0).

Warning: Be sure you know exactly *what you're doing before you try to modify the FAT entry. It's easy to cause serious problems as you modify the FAT.*

In many cases, the message that says your compressed drive is too fragmented to resize is misleading: the problem might actually be caused by a delete-tracking file located at the end of the drive. In this case, all you have to do to solve the problem is delete the file. See the section "Defrag doesn't fully defragment a drive" and the sidebar "Why Is *Mirror* So Troublesome?" a little later in this chapter.

You can't change the estimated compression ratio. If you try to change the estimated compression ratio for a compressed drive, you might receive a message indicating that the value you specified is larger than the maximum estimated compression ratio allowed for the drive.

To understand why this happens, remember that DoubleSpace uses the estimated compression ratio to determine the total capacity of the drive, and the total capacity of a compressed drive is limited to 512MB. Thus,

DoubleSpace will not let you set the estimated compression ratio to a value that would result in a drive larger than 512MB.

Suppose that your compressed drive already has 300MB of files and that there's 100MB of free space in the Compressed Volume File. An estimated compression ratio of 2.0 to 1 would cause DoubleSpace to report 200MB of free space on the drive, for a total capacity of 500MB. If you try to change the estimated compression ratio to 2.5 to 1, DoubleSpace won't let you do it because 2.5 would cause DoubleSpace to report 250MB of free space, which would make the total capacity of the drive 550MB— well beyond the 512MB maximum.

Defrag doesn't fully defragment a drive. If you receive a message indicating that you need to defragment your compressed drive and if after spending several hours defragmenting it you still receive the same message, *don't* put your fist through the monitor. I know from personal experience that this is frustrating, but there is a simple solution: the problem is most likely a hidden system unformatting file created by a delete-tracking program such as *Mirror* (MS-DOS 5 and *PC Tools*) or *Image* (*The Norton Utilities*).

Both *Mirror* and *Image* create an unformatting file at the very end of a drive. Then, they give the file the system and hidden attributes so that you can't see it in a directory listing. Unfortunately, the system attribute also prevents Defrag from moving the file. To see whether you have a *Mirror* or an *Image* unformatting file at the end of your compressed drive, use this command:

```
C:\> dir /as
```

(The /as switch stands for attribute system; it tells Dir to display all files with the system attribute.) A delete-tracking file created by *Mirror* will be named MIRORSAV.FIL; *Image* creates a file named IMAGE.IDX.

You can often avoid the Defrag step altogether if you simply delete the unformatting file. To do that, use one of these commands (depending on whether the file was created by *Mirror* or by *Image*):

```
C:\> deltree mirorsav.fil
```

or

```
C:\> deltree image.idx
```

If you don't want to delete the file, you can remove its attributes with one of these commands:

```
C:\> attrib mirorsav.fil -s -h -r
```

or

```
C:\> attrib image.idx -s -h -r
```

Then, you can defragment the drive.

You receive the message *Unrecognized error #109*. If you weren't so concerned about losing access to your compressed data, you might chuckle at the ominous error message *Unrecognized error #109*. After all, DoubleSpace obviously recognizes that there is an error, or it wouldn't be able to display an error message. And "error #109" seems pretty specific for an "unrecognized error."

Note: This error occurs only with MS-DOS 6.0. It does not occur with MS-DOS 6.2.

Fortunately, this error message has a fairly simple explanation: the Compressed Volume File itself has become excessively fragmented. There are two solutions.

You can increase the *MaxFileFragments* setting in the DBLSPACE.INI file.

If you're using MS-DOS 6.0, you must edit the DBLSPACE.INI file to change the *MaxFileFragments* setting. Here's the procedure:

1. Make the host drive the current drive.

2. Remove the attributes of the DBLSPACE.INI file with this command (assuming the host drive is H):

   ```
   H:\> attrib dblspace.ini -s -h -r
   ```

3. Start the MS-DOS Edit command or your favorite text editor.

4. Edit DBLSPACE.INI, increasing the *MaxFileFragments* value:

   ```
   MaxFileFragments=2600
   ```

Pick a value that's substantially higher than the initial value. The value *2600* is usually more than adequate.

5. Save the file and exit your editor.

Why Is *Mirror* So Troublesome?

The Mirror command can be especially troublesome for users of MS-DOS 5 who installed DoubleSpace after upgrading to MS-DOS 6.0 or 6.2. Although *Mirror* isn't included with MS-DOS 6.0 and 6.2, when you upgrade an MS-DOS 5 system to version 6.0 or 6.2, the Setup program doesn't remove MIRROR.COM from your \DOS directory. And if you added a MIRROR command to your AUTO-EXEC.BAT file, MS-DOS 6.0 and 6.2 Setup doesn't remove it.

The problem with *Mirror* is that it creates the hidden system file named MIRORSAV.FIL at the very end of your disk drive. This creates an instant fragmentation problem because there is now a large fragment of free space between the last data file on your drive and the MIRORSAV.FIL file. DoubleSpace will be unable to reduce the size of your compressed drive because the MIRORSAV.FIL file occupies the highest cluster number on the drive, so reducing the size of the drive would cause the file to be lost. DoubleSpace somewhat misleadingly tells you that the drive is too fragmented to resize.

Because the file has the system attribute, the Defrag command can't move it. So even after you've spent several hours defragmenting the drive, MIRORSAV.FIL still occupies the last cluster of the drive and the drive is thus still too fragmented to resize. The only solution is to delete the file or remove its system attribute so that Defrag can relocate it.

Image, the delete-tracking program that comes with *The Norton Utilities*, works much as *Mirror* does, creating a hidden system file named IMAGE.IDX at the end of the drive. It causes the same problems as the MIRORSAV.FIL file.

6. Restore the DBLSPACE.INI attributes:

```
H:\> attrib dblspace.ini +s +h +r
```

7. Restart your computer to activate the change.

The second solution is to defragment your Compressed Volume File. This is a little tricky, so read these instructions all the way through before you start. (Now would be a good time to do a full backup.)

1. Copy the MS-DOS files DEFRAG.EXE and ATTRIB.EXE to your uncompressed host drive (usually drive H).

2. Boot your system so that DoubleSpace won't be active. If you're using MS-DOS 6.2, restart your computer and press Ctrl+F5 when the message *Starting MS-DOS* appears. If you're using MS-DOS 6.0, temporarily rename DBLSPACE.BIN on your host drive using these commands:

```
H:\> attrib dblspace.bin -s -h -r
H:\> rename dblspace.bin dblspace.sav
```

Then, reboot your computer.

Alternatively, you can create a non-DoubleSpace system disk. First, use the command Format a: /s (the /s switch transfers the operating system to the disk). Next, use a Deltree command to delete the DBLSPACE.BIN file from the floppy disk:

```
C:\> deltree a:\dblspace.bin
```

Then, reboot your system from the new DoubleSpace-free disk you've created.

Note: Make certain DoubleSpace isn't running before you continue. If you defragment a CVF while DoubleSpace is running, you'll mangle your compressed drive. To check whether DoubleSpace is running, type mem /m dblspace *at the command prompt. You should see the message* DBLSPACE is not currently in memory.

3. Remove the attributes of the CVF with this command:

```
C:\> attrib dblspace.* -s -h -r
```

4. Run Defrag to defragment the CVF.

5. Restore the attributes of the CVF with this command:

```
C:\> attrib dblspace.* +s +h +r
```

6. If you renamed DBLSPACE.BIN on your host drive, give it its old
   name back using these commands:

```
C:\> rename dblspace.sav dblspace.bin
C:\> attrib dblspace.bin +s +h +r
```

7. Restart your computer. (If you booted from a non-DoubleSpace system disk, remove it from the drive first.)

Problems Using DoubleSpace with *Microsoft Windows*

Microsoft Windows support for DoubleSpace is unfortunately limited. You
can use compressed hard drives under *Windows*, and you can view information about compressed drives using File Manager's DoubleSpace Info
command. But you can't run the Dblspace program while *Windows* is running. While *Windows* is running, you can't create a compressed drive,
resize a compressed drive, or do any other DoubleSpace function that requires the Dblspace program.

MS-DOS 6.2 improves the usefulness of DoubleSpace with *Windows* by
providing the Automount feature so that you don't have to use the
Dblspace /mount command to access a compressed floppy disk. Aside
from this feature and the ability to use Dblspace /info or Dblspace /list
from the MS-DOS command prompt while *Windows* is running, support
for DoubleSpace in *Windows* is the same in both the MS-DOS 6.0 and 6.2
versions of DoubleSpace.

**When you start *Windows*, you receive the message *The swap
file is corrupt.*** If you receive the message *The swap file is corrupt* when
you start up *Windows*, you need to re-create the permanent swap file,
which *Windows* uses for virtual memory.

1. From the Program Manager's Main group, start up the Control Panel
   by double-clicking on its icon.

2. Double-click on the 386 Enhanced icon. *Windows* displays a dialog
   box for controlling various aspects of *Windows* operation in 386 enhanced mode.

3. Click on the Virtual Memory button. *Windows* displays a dialog box that lets you change virtual memory options. Click on the Change button.

4. In the Drive drop-down list box, choose an uncompressed drive.

5. In the Type drop-down list box, choose Permanent.

6. In the New Size box, type the size you want to use for the swap file. *Windows* suggests a size based on the amount of real memory you have and the amount of disk space that's available on the drive. This amount is usually sufficient.

For more information about the permanent swap file, see Chapter 9, "DoubleSpace and *Microsoft Windows*."

You can't access compressed drives after booting from a system disk created by File Manager. If you are to access compressed drives when you boot from a system disk, the disk must contain the DBLSPACE.BIN system file. The MS-DOS 6.0 and 6.2 Format /s command copies DBLSPACE.BIN to the disk. Unfortunately, however, File Manager's Make System Disk command on the Disk menu does not.

To boot from a system disk created by File Manager, you must first copy DBLSPACE.BIN from the \DOS directory of your C drive to the system disk, using a command like this one:

```
C:\> copy \dos\dblspace.bin a:\
```

Alternatively, you can create your system disk using the Format /s command.

SUMMARY

In this chapter, we've looked at several basic troubleshooting procedures:

- Booting clean
- Disabling DoubleSpace
- Defragmenting a compressed drive
- Resizing a compressed drive
- Scanning the disk surface for defects
- Changing settings in the DBLSPACE.INI file

In addition, we've looked at troubleshooting techniques for 16 common DoubleSpace problems in four categories:

Startup problems

- You receive the message *A CVF is damaged* when you start up your computer.

- You receive the message *Too many block devices* when you start up your computer.

- You can't access a network drive.

- An application program doesn't work after you install DoubleSpace.

- You receive a DoubleGuard alert (MS-DOS 6.2 only).

ScanDisk and CVF problems

- ScanDisk or Chkdsk reports lost allocation units.

- ScanDisk or Chkdsk reports cross-linked files.

- ScanDisk or Chkdsk reports other errors.

Disk space and fragmentation problems

- You run out of space on a compressed drive.

- You run out of space on the host drive.

- You can't reduce the size of a compressed drive.

- You can't change the estimated compression ratio.

- Defrag doesn't fully defragment a drive.

- You receive the message *Unrecognized error #109.*

Problems using DoubleSpace with *Microsoft Windows*

- When you start *Windows,* you receive the message *The swap file is corrupt.*

- You can't access compressed drives after booting from a system disk created by File Manager.

I'll double your folly.

—William Shakespeare, *Two Gentlemen of Verona*

Chapter 9

DoubleSpace and
Microsoft Windows

I have good news and bad news for *Microsoft Windows* users.

The good news is that DoubleSpace is 100 percent compatible with *Windows*. That's especially good news because *Windows* requires *lots* of disk space. Applications for *Windows* are getting bigger and bigger, and the trend shows no sign of reversing itself soon. If you're going to be a *Windows* user, you can never have enough disk space.

The bad news is that although DoubleSpace is compatible with *Windows,* it isn't fully supported by *Windows.* You must endure a few frustrating limitations when you use DoubleSpace with *Windows* because you can't run the Dblspace program while *Windows* is active. That means you can't perform some Dblspace functions, such as changing a compressed drive's size or estimated compression ratio, while *Windows* is running.

In this chapter we'll look at the few concessions *Windows* does make to DoubleSpace. Then, we'll see how to set up a *Windows* permanent swap file when DoubleSpace is used. Finally, we'll take a look at the limitations of using DoubleSpace and *Windows* together.

Note: One serious Windows *limitation with DoubleSpace in MS-DOS 6.0 was that you couldn't mount compressed floppies during a* Windows *session. This limitation made compressed floppies virtually worthless for* Windows *users. The new Automount feature of MS-DOS 6.2 changes that. Now that compressed floppies are mounted automatically when they're inserted into the drive, they're easy to use from* Windows. *In addition, MS-DOS 6.2 lets you run the Dblspace /list and Dblspace /info commands from an MS-DOS command prompt while* Windows *is running.*

FILE MANAGER'S DOUBLESPACE INFO COMMAND

When you install MS-DOS 6.0 or 6.2 on a computer with *Windows,* the MS-DOS Setup program graciously adds a new menu item, Tools, to File Manager's menu bar. This new menu contains three commands: Backup, which runs the *Microsoft Backup* program for *Windows*; Antivirus, which runs *Microsoft Anti-Virus* for *Windows*; and DoubleSpace Info, which displays information about drives compressed by DoubleSpace.

To use the DoubleSpace Info function:

1. Choose a drive by clicking on its drive icon.

2. From the File Manager's Tools menu, choose the DoubleSpace Info command. Figure 9-1 shows a typical DoubleSpace Info display.

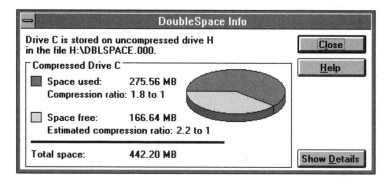

Figure 9-1. *The DoubleSpace Info display.*

Here, you can see that the host for compressed drive C is uncompressed drive H and that the Compressed Volume File's name is DBLSPACE.000. The DoubleSpace Info display also includes a pie chart that shows how much space on the drive is used and how much free space remains. Note that the free space amount is an estimate based on the estimated compression ratio.

3. Click the Show Details button to see compression information about selected files. Figure 9-2, on the next page, shows an example. For this example, I selected a range of files on the File Manager screen before I chose the DoubleSpace Info command. For each of the

selected files, DoubleSpace Info displays the file name, the size of
the file, and the file's compression ratio.

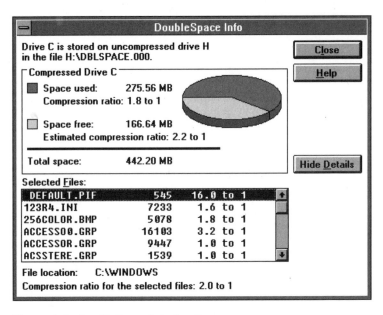

Figure 9-2. *DoubleSpace Info details.*

4. Notice in Figure 9-2 that the Show Details button has changed to a
   Hide Details button. Click this button again, and the dialog box will
   return to the shorter form shown in Figure 9-1.

DOUBLESPACE AND
THE *WINDOWS* SWAP FILE

Windows uses a *swap file* to simulate physical memory. If your computer
has only 4MB of memory, for example, *Windows* can simulate as much as
16MB by using a swap file. Whenever *Windows* runs low on real memory,
it moves inactive programs or data out to the swap file. When it needs the
program or data again, *Windows* brings it back into real memory, swap-
ping out some other program or data in its place. The simulated memory
created by the swap file is called *virtual memory.*

You can set up *Windows* to use either of two kinds of swap files: *temporary* or *permanent*. If you configure *Windows* to use a temporary swap file, *Windows* creates the swap file whenever it starts up. Then, when a *Windows* session ends, *Windows* deletes the temporary swap file. .

A permanent swap file remains on your disk even when *Windows* isn't running. It's more efficient than a temporary swap file because it is created from contiguous disk space—that is, from disk sectors that are adjacent to one another.

Unless you're very tight on disk space, it's almost always best to create a permanent swap file. However, there is a trick to creating a permanent swap file when you use DoubleSpace: the swap file must be created on an uncompressed drive. *Windows* can't use a permanent swap file that's been created on a compressed drive.

The DoubleSpace setup routine is smart enough to notice a *Windows* permanent swap file and move it to an uncompressed disk. But if you install *Windows* after installing DoubleSpace or if you didn't have a permanent swap file set up before you installed DoubleSpace, you can follow this procedure to create a permanent swap file on an uncompressed disk:

1. From the Program Manager, in the Main group, start the Control Panel by double-clicking on its icon.

2. Double-click on the 386 Enhanced icon. *Windows* displays a dialog box for controlling various aspects of *Windows* operation in 386 enhanced mode.

3. Click on the Virtual Memory button. *Windows* displays a dialog box that lets you change virtual memory options. Now click the Change button.

4. In the Drive drop-down list box, choose an uncompressed drive.

5. In the Type drop-down list box, choose Permanent.

6. In the New Size box, type the size you want to use for the swap file. *Windows* suggests a size based on the amount of real memory you have and the amount of disk space that's available on the drive. This amount is usually sufficient.

How Big Can the Swap File Be?

One confusing aspect of setting up a permanent swap file is deciding how big it should be. *Windows* tells you the maximum allowable size of the swap file and recommends a swap file size that's usually considerably smaller than the maximum. If you specify a size larger than the recommendation, you'll see this message:

```
Windows will not use more than the virtual memory
specified by the recommended size. Are you sure you want
to create a larger swap file?
```

Pay no attention to this message. It's just an example of how overzealous *Windows* can be about convincing you to take its advice. Truth is, *Windows* can use the additional virtual memory.

So how large can the swap file be? Up to four times the amount of real memory on your computer, provided you have enough free disk space to create the swap file and still leave at least 2MB of free space on the disk. For example, if you have 4MB of real memory, you can create a 16MB swap file as long as you have at least 18MB of free disk space.

For most users, a 16MB swap file is overkill, though. If you have the disk space, create a 4MB swap file. That should be adequate unless you use programs that have unusually large memory requirements.

WINDOWS LIMITATIONS

- You can't run the Dblspace program while *Windows* is active.

- With MS-DOS 6.0, compressed floppy disks aren't practical for *Windows* users. You have to mount compressed floppies using the Dblspace /mount command, and you can't use that command while *Windows* is active. That means you have to exit *Windows* every time you change disks. This is too much of a burden to bear.

  Compressed removable disks (from Bernoulli, SyQuest, and so on) are a little more practical, only because you don't change them as often as you do floppies. If you do change the cartridge, you must exit *Windows* to issue the Dblspace /mount command.

■ The MS-DOS 6.2 Automount feature is of special significance for *Windows* users since it makes using compressed floppies and removable hard disks practical. When Automount is enabled, a compressed floppy or removable hard disk is recognized and mounted automatically when it is inserted into the drive. Because you don't have to manually mount the removable compressed disk, the *Windows* restriction against running Dblspace doesn't prevent you from accessing the compressed floppy or removable disk while you're running *Windows*.

■ You can't resize a compressed drive or change its compression ratio while *Windows* is running. That's too bad because a DoubleSpace drive can often appear full when in fact it has plenty of free space; all that's needed is an adjustment to the estimated compression ratio. Unfortunately, you must exit *Windows* to make that adjustment.

SUMMARY

Windows and DoubleSpace are compatible, but DoubleSpace isn't fully supported by *Windows*.

■ *Windows* does let you use the File Manager's DoubleSpace Info command to display information about a compressed drive and compressed files.

■ The *Windows* permanent swap file must always be on an uncompressed disk.

■ Unfortunately, you can't use most Dblspace commands while *Windows* is running.

■ For MS-DOS 6.0, the restriction against using the Dblspace command while *Windows* is running makes compressed floppy disks virtually unusable. For MS-DOS 6.2, however, the Automount feature makes it easy to use both compressed floppies and removable hard disks while *Windows* is running.

This is a highly irregular procedure!

—Frank Morgan, *The Wizard of Oz*

Chapter 10

Removing DoubleSpace

You'll probably find DoubleSpace such a valuable addition to your computer that you'll soon wonder how you ever got along without it. However, if for some reason you find that you need to remove DoubleSpace, uncompressing your files, this chapter will show you how to do it.

The procedure for removing DoubleSpace depends on whether you're using MS-DOS 6.0 or 6.2. In MS-DOS 6.2, the DoubleSpace Tools menu includes an Uncompress command that removes DoubleSpace automatically. Because DoubleSpace in MS-DOS 6.0 doesn't have the Uncompress command, you'll have to follow the manual procedure outlined in this chapter if you haven't upgraded to MS-DOS 6.2.

As you read this chapter, you'll notice that you don't have to use the Format or Fdisk command to remove DoubleSpace unless you want to change the partition structure of your disk. Most users assume that removing DoubleSpace will require that they reformat their disks, and they get frustrated when they discover that DoubleSpace won't let them format a compressed C drive. Some even resort to Fdisk unnecessarily, incorrectly assuming that using Fdisk is the only way to get rid of DoubleSpace. Read this chapter, and you'll see that removing DoubleSpace isn't all that hard.

Before we start, I want to point out the obvious: you can't remove DoubleSpace if you've added more files to your compressed drive than will fit when DoubleSpace is removed and the drive is once again uncompressed. In other words, if you've compressed a 100MB drive and stored 130MB of data on it, you won't be able to remove DoubleSpace until you've trimmed your files back down to 100MB or less.

USING THE MS-DOS 6.2 DOUBLESPACE UNCOMPRESS FEATURE

If you have MS-DOS 6.2, removing DoubleSpace is relatively easy: you just use the Dblspace Uncompress command. Grab a good book. Uncompress takes time. Here's the procedure:

1. Back up everything. Removing DoubleSpace is similar to installing it, only in reverse. Although the procedure is safe, you shouldn't undertake it without first backing up your data.

2. Don't bother doing a surface analysis to check for unusable clusters before you run DoubleSpace. The Dblspace Uncompress command runs ScanDisk. Doing it yourself is just a waste of time.

3. Make sure all of your files will fit on the uncompressed drive. Run Chkdsk to find out how much disk space is occupied by the files and directories on your compressed drive. Then run Chkdsk against the host drive to find out its capacity. You don't need to include the amount of free space on the host drive in your calculations. Most of your host drive is filled by the DoubleSpace CVF, which will be removed when you remove DoubleSpace.

   If the files on the compressed drive won't fit on the uncompressed drive, you'll have to delete some of them.

4. Start DoubleSpace by typing *dblspace* at the command prompt. Then, select the drive you want to uncompress. If you have more than one compressed drive, you should uncompress all of them to completely remove DoubleSpace. When you uncompress your last compressed drive, DoubleSpace gives you the option to remove its system files from the host drive. You will have effectively removed DoubleSpace from your computer.

5. After you've selected the drive you want to uncompress, choose the Uncompress command from the Tools menu. Dblspace displays the screen shown in Figure 10-1, on the next page. To remove DoubleSpace, take a deep breath and select Yes.

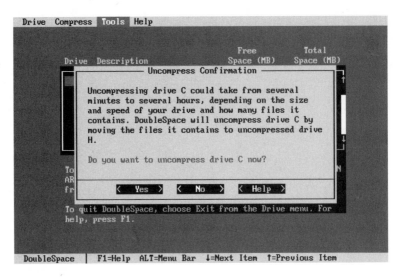

Figure 10-1. *Selecting Yes to remove DoubleSpace.*

6. DoubleSpace Uncompress starts by running ScanDisk to check for bad clusters on your host drive.

7. When ScanDisk finishes its check for bad clusters on the host, Uncompress begins to uncompress your files, displaying its progress on a screen like the one shown in Figure 10-2.

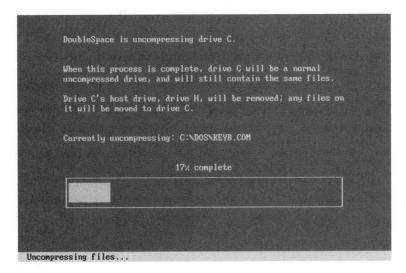

Figure 10-2. *DoubleSpace Uncompress displaying its progress.*

DoubleSpace uncompresses a drive by decompressing the drive's files and moving them to the uncompressed host drive. When it has filled the available space on the host drive, it reduces the size of the compressed drive to make additional space available on the host drive. Then, it uncompresses and moves more files. It repeats this process until all files have been uncompressed and moved.

If DoubleSpace is unable to reduce the size of the compressed drive because of fragmentation, it automatically runs the MS-DOS Defrag command to defragment the drive. When Defrag finishes, DoubleSpace Uncompress resumes.

8. When DoubleSpace Uncompress is finished uncompressing your last compressed drive, it reboots your computer. When your computer comes back up, DoubleSpace will be gone.

If you decide to activate DoubleSpace again, you can reinstall it by typing *dblspace* at the MS-DOS prompt.

REMOVING DOUBLESPACE IN MS-DOS 6.0

If you have MS-DOS 6.0, you have to use a manual procedure to remove DoubleSpace and uncompress your files. Read through the entire procedure before you start to remove DoubleSpace, and be sure you understand every step.

The procedure described here assumes that you have only one compressed drive. If you have more than one compressed drive, be sure to read the sidebar "What About Multiple Compressed Drives?" on page 143.

1. Make sure your data will fit when it's uncompressed. Start by making sure your files will fit on the uncompressed drive once DoubleSpace is removed. To find out whether they will, run the Chkdsk command on both the compressed drive and the host drive. (If you're not sure which drive is the host drive, use the Dblspace /list command to find out.) For the compressed drive, add the numbers shown for the bytes used for hidden files, directories, and user files. Then, compare this total with the number shown for the total disk space for the host drive.

If your host drive isn't large enough to hold all of your files, you'll have to get rid of some of them. Start by looking for temporary (*.TMP), backup

(*.BAK), and other files you can delete. Be sure to delete only the files you don't need to keep. If you find that you must delete important files in order to free up space, be sure to copy them to floppy disks.

Sometimes, you have to make difficult choices. If I were forced to remove DoubleSpace from my computer, I'd have to decide between keeping the word processing files for this book or my collection of Inspector Clouseau sound clips. (*Does your dog bite?*)

2. Back up your compressed drive. Next, do a complete backup of the files on your compressed drive. Ideally, you should do this backup to tape. If you don't have a tape drive and its backup software, use *Microsoft Backup* or another backup program.

This backup is not an optional step! I'm not recommending this backup just for protection in case something goes wrong. You're going to actually delete your compressed drive from its host drive and then restore the files from the backup. Without this backup, you'll be sunk.

If you're not 100 percent sure that your backups are reliable, you might want to use your backup program's Compare function immediately after finishing the backup. This function rereads the backed up data and compares it against the original to be sure the backup is reliable. It takes time, but it's worth it.

3. Copy your backup program to the host drive. In order to restore the backup of your files to the uncompressed drive, you'll need access to your backup program. So before you delete the compressed drive, copy your backup program to your uncompressed host drive.

If you backed up the compressed drive using *Microsoft Backup*, copy the MSBACKUP program files to the host drive with a command similar to this one:

```
C:\> copy \dos\msback*.* h:\dos
```

If you don't have a directory named \DOS on the host drive, create one first, using the MD command. The *Microsoft Backup* program files need about 725KB of free space on the host drive.

If you use some other backup program, copy all of its files to the host drive. Make sure the host drive has enough free space to accommodate the backup program files; if it doesn't, you might have to reduce the size of your compressed drive. If you can't create enough space on your host drive, copy the backup program to a floppy disk.

A Faster Way

You might be able to save some time by manually moving files from your compressed drive directly to your uncompressed drive. This reduces the number of files you have to back up before you delete your compressed drive. First, make the compressed drive as small as possible by using this command:

```
C:\> dblspace /size c:
```

Then, use the Xcopy command to copy files to the uncompressed host drive. For example, to copy all of the files in your \WINDOWS directory to a host drive, you'd use a command like this one:

```
C:\> xcopy \windows\*.* h:\ /s
```

Then, after checking to be sure the directory and all of its subdirectories were copied correctly, delete the \WINDOWS directory:

```
C:\> deltree \windows
```

Next, resize the compressed drive again and move more files to the host.

You can repeat this process as many times as you want. In fact, you can skip the backup and restore steps altogether if you want to. It's hard to keep track of all of your directories using this method, though. I suggest that you use it just to move your largest directories (such as \WINDOWS) and then use the backup and restore method to move the rest of the files to the uncompressed drive.

The Fastest Way to Remove DoubleSpace (Without Saving Your Compressed Files)

What if you want to get rid of DoubleSpace and you don't care about the files on your compressed drives? In that case, you can follow a more direct procedure.

Warning! This procedure is drastic! It will permanently delete all of the files on your compressed drives. Do this only if you're absolutely sure you don't want to keep those files!

1. Copy the MS-DOS COMMAND.COM file to the host drive (assuming the host is H):

   ```
   C:\> copy command.com h:\
   ```

2. Delete the DoubleSpace files from the host drive:

   ```
   C:\> deltree h:\dblspace.*
   ```

3. Restart your computer.

4. Copy COMMAND.COM to your host drive. Your host drive already contains two of the startup files required by MS-DOS: IO.SYS and MSDOS.SYS. These hidden files aren't normally displayed by the Dir command. The third file required to start MS-DOS is COMMAND.COM. Copy COMMAND.COM from your compressed C drive to your host drive using a command like this one:

```
C:\> copy command.com h:\
```

Don't copy your CONFIG.SYS and AUTOEXEC.BAT files to the host drive. They make reference to programs and device drivers that don't yet exist on your uncompressed drive.

5. Delete your DoubleSpace files. This is the scary part. First, turn to face Redmond, WA, and observe a brief moment of silence. Then, make the host drive your current drive, take a deep breath, and type this command:

```
H:\> deltree dblspace.*
```

This command takes advantage of a little-known feature of the Deltree command: it deletes files without first checking their attributes. The

DoubleSpace files have the hidden and system attributes, so you can't delete them with the usual Del command. But the Deltree command deletes even hidden and system files without hesitation.

Once you use the Deltree command, your computer is in Never-Never Land. DoubleSpace is gone from your hard drive, and the Compressed Volume File, which contained the compressed form of all your files, is gone. However, the DoubleSpace program file DBLSPACE.BIN is still active in memory, and MS-DOS still thinks you have a compressed drive C. In addition, a certain amount of data from the now-deceased C drive undoubtedly remains in internal buffers or in a disk cache if you use one. You can still make drive C your current drive, and if you use the Dir command, odds are you'll see a directory listing as if drive C still exists. Very strange.

MS-DOS has become hopelessly confused about the state of your hard disk, so it's best to proceed immediately to step 6.

What About Multiple Compressed Drives?

If you have more than one compressed drive, you should remove all but your C drive before removing DoubleSpace from your system. You can do that by backing up the files on each compressed drive, deleting the drive using the Dblspace /delete command, and then restoring the files to an uncompressed disk. (Or you can move the files from the compressed drive directly to the host drive.) Once you've removed all of your additional compressed drives, you can follow the full procedure for removing DoubleSpace.

The job is more complicated if you want to create partitions for the other drives. In that case, you'll have to back up all of your compressed drives, run Fdisk to repartition the disk, use Format to format each drive, and then restore your backups. Be sure you have a bootable floppy disk that contains FORMAT.COM and your backup, and restore software before you run Fdisk. This is a dangerous procedure, so be sure you know what you're doing before you repartition your hard disk. Good luck.

6. Reboot your computer. Press Ctrl+Alt+Del to reboot your computer. MS-DOS will restart, and what was your host drive will come up as drive C. You'll have a bare-bones configuration because your new drive C will have no CONFIG.SYS or AUTOEXEC.BAT file. Use the Dir command to check the amount of free space available on the drive.

7. Restore your backup. Now, you can change to the directory you copied your backup program to and run the backup program to restore the backup you made in step 2. (If you copied your backup program to a floppy disk, copy it to your hard disk first.)

Depending on the backup program you used, you might have to retrieve a catalog or directory file from the backup disks or tape. With Microsoft Backup, you do that by clicking the Catalog button in the Restore dialog box and then inserting the disk as prompted by the program. Other programs have a similar function.

8. Do a sanity check. You'll want to do a sanity check to make sure everything worked OK. Examine your files and directories to verify that everything is still there, and run several programs to make sure they still function. If you're a *Microsoft Windows* user, start *Windows* and check out a few programs to make sure they're still intact.

SUMMARY

DoubleSpace is easy enough to remove in MS-DOS 6.2 because of the Uncompress feature. If you must remove DoubleSpace in MS-DOS 6.0, the procedure is hair-raising:

- Make sure your data will fit when it's uncompressed.

- Back up all of your compressed files.

- Copy your backup program to the host drive.

- Copy COMMAND.COM to the root directory of the host drive.

- Delete the DBLSPACE.* files.

- Reboot.

- Restore your backup.

- Do a sanity check.

—Theme song from the TV sitcom *The Jeffersons*

Chapter 11

Converting Compressed Drives to DoubleSpace

If you already use a disk compression program such as *Stacker*, you might want to consider converting your compressed drives to DoubleSpace when you install MS-DOS 6.0 or 6.2. Because all disk compression programs use similar techniques for compressing data, DoubleSpace doesn't offer significantly more or less increase in disk space than any other program. However, it is better integrated with MS-DOS and therefore easier to use than most other disk compression programs.

If you use *Stacker* version 2.0 or 3.0, you can get a conversion disk from Microsoft for a small fee ($10 as I write this). See the sidebar "How to Get the Stacker Conversion Disk." In this chapter we'll look first at how to use that Microsoft conversion disk to automatically convert *Stacker* drives to DoubleSpace drives. Then, we'll look at a manual procedure you can use to convert other disk compression program drives to DoubleSpace drives.

USING THE STACKER CONVERSION DISK

The Stacker Conversion Disk lets you automatically convert your *Stacker*-compressed drives to DoubleSpace drives. It works by replacing the existing version of the DBLSPACE.EXE program in your \DOS directory with an updated version that contains the conversion function.

Warning: Two versions of the Stacker Conversion Disk are available, one for MS-DOS 6.0, the other for MS-DOS 6.2. Make sure you have the correct version of the conversion disk before you go on!

The conversion disk comes with detailed instructions in a file named CONVERT.TXT. Before you begin, you should print out this file using a command like this one:

```
C:\> print a:convert.txt
```

(If the conversion disk is in your B drive, type *print b:convert.txt* instead.) Read the entire CONVERT.TXT file carefully before you begin. I'm going to review the basic procedure for converting *Stacker* drives here, but the CONVERT.TXT file might have more current information.

How to Get the Stacker Conversion Disk

The only way to get Microsoft's Stacker Conversion Disk is to order it using the coupon found at the back of the *MS-DOS User's Guide.* Fill out the coupon and mail it to the address shown.

You can use the same coupon to order the MS-DOS Supplemental Disk. This disk contains several useful programs and commands that Microsoft dropped from MS-DOS 6.0 because most users never used them. If you installed MS-DOS 6.0 or 6.2 by upgrading an MS-DOS 5 system, you already have all of the supplemental programs, so you don't need the Supplemental Disk. But if you upgraded from an earlier version of MS-DOS, or if you installed MS-DOS 6.0 or 6.2 on a new system (or bought a new system with MS-DOS 6.0 or 6.2 already installed), you might find the Supplemental Disk useful.

You can also use the coupon to order the MS-DOS 6.0 and 6.2 Resource Kit, which comes with the Supplemental Disk and a 358-page *Technical Reference* that contains, among other things, a detailed reference to MS-DOS 6.0 and 6.2 commands and a 52-page section on DoubleSpace.

Here's the basic procedure for converting *Stacker* drives to DoubleSpace drives. Insert the conversion disk into a floppy drive, make that drive the current drive, and type this command:

```
A:\> convert
```

This command runs a batch file, CONVERT.BAT, that copies the new version of the DBLSPACE.EXE program to your hard disk and then runs the new version to automatically convert your *Stacker* drives.

CONVERT.BAT also creates a batch file named CLEANUP.BAT. After the conversion is finished, you should run CLEANUP.BAT to delete any leftover files that were created during the conversion process but are no longer necessary.

Although *Stacker* conversion is automatic, it sometimes stops if it runs into trouble, such as not enough memory or disk space. If that happens, just correct the problem and run Convert again. Here are a few things you can do up front to make the conversion run smoothly:

- Clean up your *Stacker* drives by deleting any unnecessary files.

- Free up as much space on your host drives as possible.

- If you're using *Stacker* version 3.0, shrink your *Stacker* drives to make them as small as possible.

- Run Scheck on your *Stacker* drives and correct any errors it finds.

- Free up as much conventional memory as possible. Edit your CONFIG.SYS and AUTOEXEC.BAT, and add the word REM (followed by a space) before any line that loads a memory-resident program or device driver that isn't absolutely necessary for your computer to function. (*Don't* REM the lines that load the *Stacker* device drivers such as STACKER.COM or SSWAP.COM, or the lines that load MS-DOS into high memory: *Dos=high,umb*, *Device=c:\dos\emm386.exe*, and *Device=c:\dos\himem.sys*.)

One final word of warning: *Stacker* conversion is s-l-o-w. We're talking start-it-on-Friday-and-let-it-run-over-the-weekend slow. I once converted two 100MB *Stacker* drives on a 16MHz 386 system. I left the conversion well under way at 6:00 one evening and returned to the office at 7:30 the next morning. The display said it was 80 percent done. It took another two hours or so. Yawn.

Because the *Stacker* conversion program is so slow, you might want to consider using the manual procedure described later in this chapter—especially if you have a tape drive, which makes it a lot easier to back up and restore your compressed data.

Converting *Stacker* Floppies

When the *Stacker* conversion process finishes, you're left with an updated version of the Dblspace program that includes a new command in its Tools menu: Convert Stacker. You can use this command at any time to convert other *Stacker* drives, such as those on floppy disks, to DoubleSpace.

CONVERT.BAT: The Zaniest Batch File Ever

If you like complicated batch files, take a look at CONVERT.BAT. You'll love it.

The CONVERT.BAT file demonstrates a number of far-out batch file programming techniques. When you run CONVERT.BAT, it calls a batch file named GETPATH, which looks through the directories in your search path to find the file DBLSPACE.EXE. Then CONVERT.BAT restarts itself, this time specifying the complete directory path for DBLSPACE.EXE as a command-line parameter.

The second time through, CONVERT.BAT looks for the *Stacker* Check or Scheck command. Then CONVERT.BAT restarts itself again, this time passing the directory path for DBLSPACE.EXE and the directory path for CHECK.EXE or SCHECK.EXE as command-line parameters.

The third time through, CONVERT.BAT displays a Welcome message and asks you if you want to continue. Then it copies the new version of DBLSPACE.EXE to the directory specified in the first parameter, runs Check or Scheck (depending on the second parameter) to check every *Stacker* drive, creates a batch file named CLEANUP.BAT, and finally runs the updated DBLSPACE com-

Unfortunately, a *Stacker*-compressed disk must contain at least 900KB of free space if it is to be converted using the Dblspace Convert Stacker command. That means that the floppy disk must be significantly less than half full. The CONVERT.TXT file documents a rather confusing procedure you can follow to convert a floppy disk that has less than 900KB of free space. It works by copying the *Stacker* Compressed Volume File to your hard disk and converting it there:

1. Insert the floppy disk in your disk drive.

2. Move the STACVOL.DSK file from your floppy disk to your host drive. The STACVOL.DSK file is *Stacker*'s equivalent of DoubleSpace's Compressed Volume File. You need to change the

mand to convert the *Stacker* drives. The batch file command that actually runs DBLSPACE is

```
%1
```

The *%1* command will work because a previous iteration of the CONVERT.BAT file specified the complete file-spec for the Dblspace command as a command-line parameter.

How does CONVERT.BAT manage to keep track of where it is when it restarts itself? By counting command-line parameters. The first time through, when you start CONVERT.BAT from the command line, there are no command-line parameters. The second time, after CONVERT.BAT has restarted itself, there is one parameter: the complete path for the DBLSPACE.EXE file. The third time, after CONVERT.BAT has restarted itself again, there are two parameters: the path for DBLSPACE.EXE and the path for CHECK.EXE or SCHECK.EXE.

For more hair-raising batch file thrills, try to figure out how the GETPATH.BAT batch file works. And see if you can figure out what the Allstack command does. Bother.

file name extension from .DSK to .001 when you move the file, so you'll want to use a command similar to this one:

```
C:\> move a:stacvol.dsk h:\stacvol.001.
```

Check the size of the STACVOL.DSK file first, and make sure you have enough room for it on your host drive. If you don't, you'll have to shrink your compressed drive to free up additional space on your host drive.

3. Convert the *Stacker* Compressed Volume File to DoubleSpace by using a command like this one:

```
C:\> dblspace /convstac=h:stacvol.001
```

After DoubleSpace converts the CVF, it will mount it. Make a note of the drive letter it uses for the CVF mount. In this example, I'll assume it mounts the converted CVF's drive as drive I.

4. Delete everything from the floppy disk using this command:

```
C:\> deltree a:*.*
```

The Deltree command will prompt you to confirm that each file is to be deleted; just press Y each time. (If the floppy disk contains any uncompressed files you want to keep, move them from the disk before deleting everything.)

5. Compress the floppy disk using a command like this one:

```
C:\> dblspace /compress a:
```

DoubleSpace will mount the compressed drive as A, picking another drive letter for the compressed floppy's host.

6. Copy all of the files from the converted compressed drive (drive I) to the compressed floppy drive (drive A):

```
C:\> xcopy i:*.* a: /s
```

7. Delete the converted compressed drive (drive I) with a Dblspace command like this one:

```
C:\> dblspace /delete i:
```

Is There a New Version of DBLSPACE.EXE?

When you run Convert, it copies a new version of DBLSPACE.EXE to your \DOS directory. The only difference between this version and the standard version is that the new version includes the *Stacker* conversion routines.

Early on in the life of MS-DOS 6.0, a rumor that Microsoft had secretly released a bug fix for DoubleSpace started up. The rumor was based on the fact that some users had a DBLSPACE.EXE file with a different time stamp and file size than other users had. Users incorrectly assumed that the more current DBLSPACE.EXE was an updated version that included a bug fix. In reality, the more current version was found only on systems on which the Stacker Conversion Disk had been used.

CONVERTING DRIVES COMPRESSED BY OTHER PROGRAMS TO DOUBLESPACE

If you use a compression program other than *Stacker,* you'll have to follow a manual procedure for converting your compressed drives to DoubleSpace drives. This manual conversion procedure is described in the README.TXT file that comes with MS-DOS 6.0 and 6.2. Be sure to read it over carefully before you start.

1. Install MS-DOS 6.0 or 6.2 if you haven't already.

2. Back up your compressed drives using *Microsoft Backup* or another high-speed backup program. If you have a tape drive, use it—with its own backup software. If you have important files on an uncompressed drive, back them up too. And if you use a program other than *Microsoft Backup,* make sure you have a copy of it on floppy disk. Make a copy now if you don't.

3. Create a bootable floppy disk by inserting a blank disk in drive A and typing this command:

```
C:\> format a: /s
```

Then, copy the Format command to the disk:

```
C:\> copy \dos\format.com a:
```

Finally, press Ctrl+Alt+Del to boot from this disk.

Note: If your MS-DOS 6.0 or 6.2 setup disks are compatible with your A drive, you can boot from the MS-DOS Setup Disk 1 without creating your own bootable floppy.

4. Use the Format command to format your host drive. If you're not sure which drive is the host drive, consult the manual that came with your disk compression software. If the host drive is your startup drive (that is, drive C before any drive letters are swapped), use the /s switch on the Format command to transfer the operating system files to it.

5. If you have MS-DOS 6.0, use a surface analysis program such as *The Norton Utilities* or *PC Tools* to scan your disk for surface defects. If you have MS-DOS 6.2, the DoubleSpace Setup routine will automatically run the new ScanDisk program to perform a surface analysis, so you can skip this step.

6. Insert the MS-DOS 6.0 or 6.2 Setup Disk 1 into drive A or B and type *a:setup* or *b:setup* at the command prompt. Then follow the instructions on the screen.

7. When Setup finishes, install DoubleSpace by typing *dblspace* at the command prompt. Then follow the instructions on the screen.

8. Restore the files you backed up in step 2. You'll probably have to retrieve the catalog or directory file from the disk or the tape. You might also have to reconfigure the backup program.

SUMMARY

Although it's not easy, it is possible to convert drives compressed by other disk compression programs to DoubleSpace drives.

■ You can convert *Stacker*-compressed drives using the Stacker Conversion Disk available from Microsoft.

- You can also use the Stacker Conversion Disk to convert *Stacker*-compressed floppy disks.

- You have to use a manual procedure to convert drives compressed by other disk compression programs to DoubleSpace drives.

- Because the *Stacker* conversion program is so slow, you might want to use the manual procedure to convert even *Stacker*-compressed drives, especially if you have a tape drive for backup.

I will decide what is ridiculous.

—Chief Inspector J. Clouseau, *A Shot in the Dark*

Chapter 12

Enhancing DoubleSpace Use with Third-Party Utilities

Several companies market DoubleSpace-compatible products you can use to get features you don't find in DoubleSpace, to intensify the effects of DoubleSpace, to supplement several DoubleSpace features, and to enhance DoubleSpace use with *Microsoft Windows* and with floppy disks.

In this chapter we'll survey several third-party utility programs: Vertisoft's *SpaceMan;* Addstor's *DoubleTools;* Symantec's *The Norton Utilities, Version 7*; and Central Point Software's *PC Tools Pro.*

Other DoubleSpace-compatible utilities are bound to pop up, so stay alert!

SPACEMAN

Vertisoft describes *SpaceMan* as "the Perfect Data Compression Utility for MS-DOS 6 DoubleSpace." They might be overstating the case just a bit, but *SpaceMan* does provide several features that are conspicuously missing from DoubleSpace.

SelectCompress

SpaceMan's *SelectCompress* feature lets you control the degree of compression for various types of files. You can choose from among four degrees of compression:

- *DOS* is the same as the compression provided by DoubleSpace.

- *Ultra I* compresses files noticeably more than standard DOS compression does but at the cost of slightly slower performance. If you have a fast 386 or better processor, you probably won't notice much of a speed difference between DOS and Ultra I.

- *Ultra II* compresses files even more than Ultra I, but with a severe loss of performance. Ultra II is best used for program files, which are usually written to disk only once but are read many times. Although it takes longer to compress a file using Ultra I and Ultra II, those files can be read and decompressed as fast as files compressed with standard DOS compression.

- *None* is used for files that are already in a compressed format, such as files compressed by *PKZIP*. Since these files have already been compressed, there's no point in trying to compress them further.

You assign one of these compression levels to four different types of files:

- *Text files* are document files created by your word processor, spreadsheet, database, or other application program. Text files are read and written frequently as you use your computer. For the best performance, you should specify DOS as the compression level for text files. If you have an exceptionally fast computer, you might want to specify Ultra I to save additional disk space.

- *Binary files* are executable program files. Binary files are read frequently but aren't often written. For maximum disk savings, specify Ultra II for your binary files. This level of compression will significantly slow your computer when you write the files, but the files aren't often written anyway.

  Note: If you're a programmer, you probably do write binary files frequently. In that case, you should specify DOS or Ultra I for your binary files.

- *Compressed files* are files that have already been compressed by a compression program such as *PKZIP*. Specify None for these files.

- *Other files* are files that don't fit any of the other three categories. Specify DOS or Ultra I for these files.

SpaceMan's SelectCompress determines the category each file on a compressed drive belongs to based on the file's extension. You can customize the extensions assigned to each category.

SuperCompress

SuperCompress is a *SpaceMan* feature that lets you compress the files on an existing compressed drive using *SpaceMan*'s Ultra II compression level. This extreme level of compression can result in a significant increase in compression for most types of files. While SelectCompress changes the compression level used for files whenever they are written to disk, SuperCompress is a batch-compression feature: it supercompresses all of the files on your compressed drive (or selected files, if you wish) in a batch, often tying up your computer for hours while it works. It's the kind of program feature you let run overnight or better yet during a weekend trip to Disneyland.

SuperMount

SpaceMan's *SuperMount* feature is similar to the MS-DOS 6.2 Automount feature: it automatically mounts a compressed floppy disk or a removable hard disk when you insert the disk in the drive. Like Automount, *SpaceMan*'s SuperMount feature can be disabled or it can be enabled only for certain drives.

SuperExchange

SpaceMan's *SuperExchange* feature lets you access a compressed floppy disk with a computer that doesn't have the DoubleSpace utility on it. SuperExchange does this by copying a special program called Superx to the uncompressed part of a compressed floppy disk. In order to access the compressed data when you're using a computer that doesn't have DoubleSpace, you insert the floppy disk in the drive and run the Superx program. Superx mounts the compressed disk so that the non-DoubleSpace computer can access it. SuperExchange works on any computer running MS-DOS 3.3 or later.

FortuneTeller

As you know, DoubleSpace calculates the amount of free space on your disk using an estimated compression ratio. Unfortunately, there's no guarantee that the estimated compression ratio is accurate. *SpaceMan's FortuneTeller* is a memory resident program that reports free disk space based on the actual compression ratio already achieved for files on your disk. In some cases, this report gives you a more accurate estimate of free disk space.

Space Monitor

Space Monitor is the information part of the *SpaceMan* window displayed from MS-DOS or *Microsoft Windows*. Figure 12-1 shows the *Windows* version.

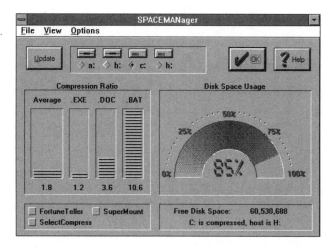

Figure 12-1. SpaceMan's *Space Monitor feature displaying information about your compressed drives.*

The information Space Monitor displays includes

- The Disk Space Usage graph, which shows speedometer-style how full the selected drive is.

- The four Compression Ratio graphs, which show bar-chart style the average compression ratio for all the files on the disk plus the ratios for files with three common extensions: .EXE, .DOC, and .BAT. You can easily change the extensions displayed in these graphs.

- The three check boxes at the bottom left of the window, which indicate whether the FortuneTeller, SuperMount, and SelectCompress features are activated.

- At the bottom right of the window, the amount of disk space free on the current drive and the compressed drive's host drive letter.

To display information for a different drive, just click on the drive's icon near the top left of the screen. To update the display, click on the Update button. And to exit *SpaceMan*, click on the OK button.

DOUBLETOOLS

DoubleTools, from Addstor, Inc., lets you manage your compressed drives from within *Microsoft Windows.* It doesn't let you create compressed hard drives or remove compressed hard drives from within *Windows,* but it does let you manage most other aspects of DoubleSpace operation from within *Windows. DoubleTools* has three main modules: Compression Central, File Director, and RescueTools.

Compression Central

Compression Central is the *DoubleTools* program that lets you manage DoubleSpace from within the *Windows* environment. You activate Compression Central's various functions by clicking on the buttons that appear in a row across the bottom of the screen. Figure 12-2 shows the Compression Central window with the SpaceGauge function activated.

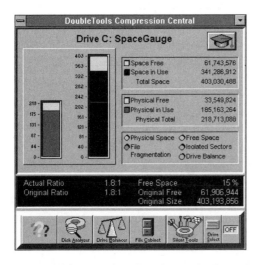

Figure 12-2. Compression Central*'s SpaceGauge feature.*

- *SpaceGauge* displays information about the space used by a compressed drive. Its left bar chart shows the actual space taken up by the CVF, and its second bar chart shows the estimated amount of compressed free space available. Its "warning lights" glow green, yellow, or red to indicate the status of various free space gauges.

- *Disk Analyzer* analyzes the degree of file fragmentation on a drive and lets you optionally launch a defragmenter program that defragments your drive in the background so that you can continue to work.

- *Drive Balancer* lets you manipulate the estimated compression ratio and CVF size while *Windows* is running. Normally, you'd have to exit *Windows* to change these settings.

- *File Cabinet* provides quick access to some basic file operations, such as viewing, copying, or deleting files.

- *Silent Tools* lets you defragment your files or scan your compressed data for structural errors in the background, while you continue with other work.

- *Drive Select* lets you mount or unmount drives or create compressed floppy disks while *Windows* is running. When you create a compressed floppy disk, you can include a feature called *Universal Data Exchange* (*UDE*), which enables a system without DoubleSpace (or without *DoubleTools,* for that matter) to access data on the compressed floppy. This is similar to *SpaceMan*'s SuperExchange feature.

File Director

File Director is the *DoubleTools* advanced file management utility that lets you manipulate files in unusual ways:

- File Director can create a *Spanned Media Drive* (*SMD*—the Addstor people seem to love acronyms). An SMD is a set of floppy disks that looks like a single compressed drive. You can copy a bunch of files that wouldn't fit on one floppy disk to an SMD, and *DoubleTools* will prompt you to insert the right disk whenever necessary.

- File Director includes a feature called *Data Transporter* that bundles a group of files into a single executable file you can send to another user over a network or a modem link (or even via the Sneaker Net). The other user then runs the program, and *voilà!*—a new drive appears that contains the files that were sent. You can think of this feature as the DoubleSpace equivalent of *PKZIP*'s self-extracting file feature.

Rescue Tools

Rescue Tools is the *DoubleTools* disk repair program you run from the command line. You can't run it from *Windows*. Rescue Tools is similar to the MS-DOS 6.2 ScanDisk program, except that it doesn't perform a surface analysis to check for defects.

THE NORTON UTILITIES, VERSION 7

The Norton Utilities has set the standard in data recovery utilities for years. Version 7 fully supports DoubleSpace drives as well as compressed drives created by *Stacker* and *SuperStor*.

- *Norton Disk Doctor* (*NDD*) now checks the internal structure of a DoubleSpace CVF, much as the MS-DOS 6.2 ScanDisk program does. For DoubleSpace drives, NDD checks both the compressed drive and the host drive.

- *The Norton Utilities* disk defragmenter, *Speed Disk*, defragments compressed drives in two stages. First, it defragments the files stored in the compressed drive. Then, it defragments the internal structure of the CVF. Unlike Defrag, however, Speed Disk doesn't do that by running the slow Dblspace /defrag command. Instead, it uses its own CVF defragmenting routines. The result is much faster operation.

- Version 7 of *The Norton Utilities* comes with a new cache program called *NCACHE2*. NCACHE2 is 100 percent compatible with DoubleSpace.

PC TOOLS PRO

At the time I wrote this book, Central Point Software was readying a new version of its popular package of utility programs, *PC Tools*. The new version will be known as *PC Tools Pro*. All of the programs that come with *PC Tools Pro* are compatible with DoubleSpace, and several of them provide features specifically designed for DoubleSpace drives.

- Like ScanDisk and *The Norton Utilities* NDD program, the *PC Tools* disk repair program, *DiskFix* now checks the internal structure of a DoubleSpace CVF. For DoubleSpace drives, DiskFix checks both the compressed drive and the host drive.

- The disk defragmenter that comes with *PC Tools* is called *Optimizer*. Like *The Norton Utilities* Speed Disk, Optimizer defragments compressed drives in two stages: first, it defragments the FAT structures, and then it defragments the compressed data stored in the CVF. And like Speed Disk, Optimizer avoids DoubleSpace's own Defrag function, with greater speed as a result.

- The disk cache for *PC Tools Pro*, *PC-Cache*, is fully compatible with DoubleSpace.

SUMMARY

There aren't a lot of utility programs that support DoubleSpace yet, but there probably will be soon.

- *SpaceMan* adds several useful features to DoubleSpace, most notably the ability to apply a higher degree of compression to certain files.

- *DoubleTools* also adds several useful features to DoubleSpace. Its most notable feature is its ability to manipulate a compressed drive's size and compression ratio from *Windows*.

- *The Norton Utilities, Version 7*, brings its well-known disk repair capabilities to bear on DoubleSpace drives.

- *PC Tools Pro* also extends its familiar disk utilities to handle DoubleSpace drives.

I gots to know...
                        —Dirty Harry

Chapter 13

Inside DoubleSpace

Some people are content knowing how to use a computer. Others aren't; they lie awake at night wondering how it works. If that sounds like you, you're going to like this chapter. We're going to pop the hood and look inside DoubleSpace to see how it works. Roll up your sleeves, and prepare to get some grease under your fingernails. This is going to be fun.

In this chapter, we'll look at five aspects of the inner workings of DoubleSpace:

- The Microsoft Real-Time Compression Interface (MRCI), a standard for data compression Microsoft developed for DoubleSpace.

- The internal format of a Compressed Volume File (CVF), which contains the data for a compressed drive.

- How DoubleSpace affects the way your computer boots.

- DBLSPACE.INI, a text file that contains startup parameters for DoubleSpace.

- The DoubleSpace System Application Programming Interface (API), which provides several functions an application program can use to examine and manipulate data in a DoubleSpace CVF.

If you're a programmer, you'll especially appreciate the information in this chapter. However, you won't find enough information here to write programs that manipulate DoubleSpace volumes. After all, this isn't a programming book. For the kind of excruciatingly detailed information you need to write utility programs that directly manipulate DoubleSpace CVFs, consult the *Microsoft MS-DOS Programmer's Reference 6.0* (Microsoft Press, 1993).

Even if you're not a programmer, this chapter will give you countless insights into DoubleSpace. The more you know about how DoubleSpace works, the better you'll be able to put it to good use.

MICROSOFT REAL-TIME COMPRESSION INTERFACE

You may have heard that the new Microsoft Backup program (Msbackup) uses DoubleSpace to compress data as it writes it to disk. Strictly speaking, Msbackup doesn't use DoubleSpace for data compression. Instead, Msbackup and DoubleSpace share a common data compression technology called *MRCI,* for *Microsoft Real-Time Compression Interface.*

MRCI provides a standard for data compression. It spells out the details of how data is compressed and provides a standard programming interface for calling the routines that compress and decompress data. In addition, Microsoft provides a basic MRCI function library to software developers who want to develop compression software that's compatible with MRCI.

MRCI's compression routines can be incorporated directly into a program (as they are with DoubleSpace and Msbackup), or they can be loaded into memory as a memory resident program called an *MRCI server.* Then, the MRCI server provides compression services for any program that requires them. A program that uses an MRCI server is called an *MRCI client.*

How Do You Say MRCI?

Without doubt the most controversial aspect of DoubleSpace is the proper pronunciation of the acronym MRCI. Those who studied English too hard in grade school spell out the letters: *Em-Are-See-Aye.* Those who want people to think they know more about it than they really do pronounce it *Mercy.* The hip crowd gives it a French twist, pronouncing it *Mercí.* (This is acceptable only if spoken with a heavy Clouseau accent.) Texans generally call it *Marci,* and devotees of *Stacker* have been known to pronounce it *Murky.*

Even though Microsoft provides an MRCI function library, software developers might figure out ways to write more efficient MRCI servers. If you were to load a more efficient MRCI server into memory, DoubleSpace and Msbackup would use it instead of the Microsoft routines.

In fact, MRCI provides for the possibility that the compression routines could be implemented by dedicated hardware. For example, you might in the near future be able to buy a 32-bit VESA Local Bus MRCI server for $149. (Well, they probably won't be that cheap at first. But they'll get there.) And who knows, someday an MRCI server might even be built into the microprocessor chip!

A hardware-based MRCI server would have at least these three advantages: faster performance, better compression, and smaller memory requirements.

INSIDE A COMPRESSED VOLUME FILE

As you already know, the data for a compressed DoubleSpace drive is stored on the host drive in a special file called a *Compressed Volume File,* or *CVF*. When DoubleSpace mounts a compressed drive, it fools MS-DOS into thinking that the CVF is actually a separate drive. To understand how it is able to do that, you need to know a little about the internal structure of a CVF.

Compressed Volume Files are named according to this model:

> DBLSPACE.*nnn*

where *nnn* is a three-digit sequence number. When you compress the existing data on a drive, the sequence number 000 is assigned to the CVF. When you create empty compressed drives, sequence numbers are sequentially assigned starting with 001. In theory, the highest allowable sequence number is 254. You'd be crazy to create that many compressed drives, though.

Inside the CVF, DoubleSpace stores data in compressed form (using MRCI to actually perform the compression). DoubleSpace also allocates space to disk files using variable-length clusters rather than fixed-length clusters. To maintain compatibility with MS-DOS application programs, DoubleSpace simulates a standard MS-DOS drive. As a result, a compressed drive looks like an ordinary uncompressed drive to you and your application programs. But internally, the structure of a compressed drive is quite different from the structure of an uncompressed drive.

Figure 13-1 is an overview of the internal structure of a CVF. As you can see, it contains several new structures in addition to the traditional FAT and root directory. (This is *not* a precise layout of the CVF; I've omitted a few parts that aren't significant to this discussion. For more complete information about the CVF structure, consult the *Microsoft MS-DOS Programmer's Reference 6.0.*)

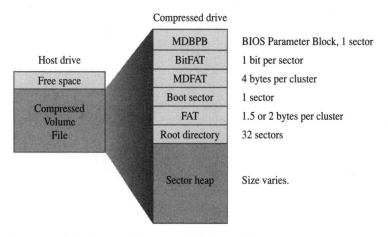

Figure 13-1. *Inside a Compressed Volume File.*

I'll explain each of these CVF structures here, but not in the order in which they appear in Figure 13-1.

The Root Directory

The root directory in a CVF is identical to the root directory on a standard MS-DOS disk. It contains 512 directory entries, each of which is 32 bytes long. As a result, the root directory occupies 32 sectors.

Each 32-byte root directory entry contains the following fields:

Offset	Length	Contents
0	11	The complete file name consisting of an 8-byte name and a 3-byte extension.
11	1	The attribute field. The various bits of this field are used to indicate whether the entry is a read-only file, a hidden file, a system file, a volume label, or a subdirectory. In addition, the attribute field contains the archive bit, which is used to manage incremental backups.
12	10	Reserved for use by MS-DOS.
22	2	The time stamp.
24	2	The date stamp.
26	2	The starting cluster number for the file. The value of this field corresponds to the FAT entry for the file's first cluster.
28	4	The file length.

Subdirectory entries have the same format as root directory entries, but subdirectories aren't limited to 512 directory entries.

The File Allocation Table

Like the root directory, the File Allocation Table (FAT) for a compressed drive is identical to the FAT for an uncompressed drive. It contains one entry for each cluster in the drive. For DoubleSpace compressed drives, each cluster always represents 16 sectors.

The value stored in each FAT entry represents the status of the corresponding cluster:

Value	Meaning
(0)000h	The cluster is free.
(0)001h	This value is not used.
(F)FF0h–(F)FF6h	These values are reserved.
(F)FF7h	The cluster is unreadable and should not be used.
(F)FF8h–(F)FFFh	The cluster is the file's last cluster.
Any other value	The cluster is allocated to a file. The value represents the next cluster that is allocated to the same file.

(These values are in hexadecimal notation. That's why they contain *F*s.)

The clusters that belong to a particular file are chained together by their FAT entries. MS-DOS uses the file's directory entry to locate the file's first cluster. Then, it looks at each FAT entry to locate the other clusters that belong to the file. For example, the second FAT entry for a file points to the third FAT entry, which points to the fourth entry, and so on. The chain continues until a FAT entry with a value in the range *(F)FF8h* through *(F)FFFh,* which marks the end of the file, is encountered.

The FAT for a compressed floppy disk is a bit different. As a compressed hard disk does, a compressed floppy disk uses 8KB clusters. However, the FAT for a floppy uses only 12 bits per entry rather than 16. A 12-bit FAT can theoretically have no more than 4096 clusters. At 8KB per cluster, this limits the theoretical capacity of a 12-bit FAT to 32MB—far more than you're likely to store on a floppy disk.

The MDFAT

In a DoubleSpace compressed drive, the FAT is the primary record keeping structure for recording which clusters belong to a given file. Each cluster represents 16 sectors of uncompressed data. However, DoubleSpace uses an additional structure called the *Microsoft DoubleSpace File Allocation Table,* or *MDFAT,* to keep track of how the uncompressed data for each cluster is stored in compressed form within the CVF.

The MDFAT is twice as large as the FAT: its entries are 4 bytes each. Because each MDFAT entry provides additional information about the cluster represented by its corresponding FAT entry, you can think of the MDFAT as an extension to the standard FAT.

Each MDFAT entry contains the following information about a cluster:

Bits	Description
0–20	The number of the first sector in the sector heap that stores data for this cluster, minus 1. For example, if this value is *2000*, the first sector for the cluster is sector 2001. (The sector heap is the area of the CVF that stores compressed data. It's described next.)
21	Reserved; always *0*.

(continued)

continued

Bits	Description
22–25	The number of sectors used to store data for this cluster, minus 1. For example, if the value is *7*, then 8 sectors are used for this cluster. For a full 16-sector uncompressed cluster, the data in the cluster is compressed to half its original size (a 2.0 to 1 ratio).
26–29	The number of sectors used to store the uncompressed data for this cluster, minus 1. For most clusters, this value is *15*, meaning that the data in the cluster requires 16 sectors. Because the last cluster allocated to a file may be a partial cluster, this value can be less than *15*.
30	Indicates whether the data for this cluster is stored in compressed form (*0*) or uncompressed form (*1*). If DoubleSpace is unable to compress the data enough to save at least 1 sector, the cluster is stored uncompressed.
31	Indicates whether the cluster is in use (*1*) or is unused (*0*).

The MDFAT is the structure that lets DoubleSpace allocate disk space to files 1 sector at a time rather than a full cluster at a time. In effect, the MDFAT supports variable-length clusters. Instead of each cluster being an arbitrary 16 sectors long, DoubleSpace allocates only as many sectors as are needed to store each cluster in compressed form. Then, it records the actual length of the cluster in the MDFAT entry.

The Sector Heap

One of the major differences between a compressed drive and an uncompressed drive is that with an uncompressed drive, the sectors used for FAT clusters are laid out on the disk in a neat row. If each cluster has 16 sectors, the first 16 sectors following the root directory are cluster 1, the next 16 are cluster 2, and so on. It's easy to calculate the sector number for a given cluster: you just multiply the cluster number by the number of sectors in each cluster and add an offset to account for the FAT and the root directory.

Not so with DoubleSpace. Since each cluster is variable in length, the sectors used for clusters can't be lined up neatly in a row. Instead, DoubleSpace pools all of the available sectors in a CVF into what it calls the *sector heap*. You can think of the sector heap as, well, a heap of sectors. Whenever DoubleSpace needs to allocate sectors for a cluster, it rummages through the heap until it finds a set of contiguous free sectors. Then, it marks those sectors as in-use and records the starting sector number in the MDFAT.

A natural consequence of the way DoubleSpace allocates sectors is that a compressed drive is more prone to fragmentation than an uncompressed drive. To see why, consider what happens when you delete a file whose compression ratio is 4.0 to 1. This file uses only 4 sectors per cluster. If the file is fragmented, you might well leave numerous small fragments of available space that are only 4 sectors long when you delete it. These sectors can be used only by other clusters that compress to 4 sectors.

When you defragment a compressed drive, DoubleSpace moves all of the available free sectors to the end of the sector heap, eliminating small and often unusable fragments of free space. That's why it's important to periodically defragment your compressed drives.

The first sector of each compressed cluster contains a 4-byte *compression tag* that indicates the degree of compression that's been applied to the cluster:

Tag (in hex)	Meaning
44 53 00 00	Level 2 compression
44 53 00 01	Maximum compression
44 53 00 02	Standard compression
44 53 00 03	Level 3 compression
44 53 00 04	Level 4 compression

The compression tag makes it possible for future versions of DoubleSpace or for utilities like *SpaceMan* to provide varying degrees of compression. DoubleSpace currently uses only standard compression, except of course for clusters that can't be compressed at all.

An uncompressed cluster is stored without a compression tag. However, because it's possible that an uncompressed cluster could begin with a value that looks like a valid compression tag, the MDFAT compression bit (bit 30) is always checked to determine whether or not a cluster is compressed. If the MDFAT indicates that the cluster is compressed, the compression tag can then be checked to determine the compression level.

The BitFAT

To efficiently search the sector heap to find available sectors, Double-Space uses yet another structure called the *Bit-mapped File Allocation Table,* or *BitFAT.* The BitFAT is a simple table that contains 1 bit for every sector in the sector heap. If a sector is free, its bit in the BitFAT is set to *0.* If the sector is used, its bit is set to *1.* DoubleSpace can quickly find available sectors by scanning the BitFAT.

For a 512MB drive (the largest possible DoubleSpace drive), the size of the BitFAT is 128KB, or 256 sectors.

Whenever you restart your computer or mount a compressed drive, DoubleSpace scans the MDFAT and completely rebuilds the BitFAT. As it scans the MDFAT, it checks for errors. If you receive the message *A CVF is damaged* when you start your computer, it's because DoubleSpace found an error in the MDFAT while rebuilding the BitFAT. Run Chkdsk (MS-DOS 6.0) or ScanDisk (MS-DOS 6.2) to correct the error.

The MDBPB

The first sector (sector 0) of every standard MS-DOS disk contains a *BIOS Parameter Block,* or *BPB.* This structure contains information that describes the characteristics of the drive, such as how many bytes per sector, how many sectors per cluster, the total number of clusters on the drive, and so on. MS-DOS depends on this critical information to properly access the data on the drive.

The first sector of every CVF contains a similar structure, called the *Microsoft DoubleSpace BIOS Parameter Block,* or *MDBPB.* This structure contains an MS-DOS compatible BPB plus a set of extensions that provide information that's unique to DoubleSpace drives. Most of these extension fields are used to provide the size and location of the other structures in the CVF. For example, the field named *secHeapStart* provides the starting sector number for the sector heap, the area of the CVF from which DoubleSpace allocates sectors to your files. Figure 13-2 shows a C-language definition of the MDBPB.

One of the more interesting fields in the MDBPB is the last one, *cmbCVFMax.* This field contains the maximum size in megabytes of the CVF. When DoubleSpace creates a CVF, it sets the *cmbCVFMax* field to

```
/*** MDBPB -- Compressed Volume File "BIOS Parameter Block"
 *
 *   This structure appears in the first sector of a Compressed
 *   Volume File and contains information that describes the
 *   size and location of the remaining parts of the CVF.
 */

typedef struct { /* mp */

    char   jmpBOOT[3];        // Jump to bootstrap routine
    char   achOEMName[8];     // OEM Name ("MSDSP6.0")

    /*
     * The following fields clone an MS-DOS BPB.
     */
    short  cbPerSec;          // No. of bytes per sector (always 512)
    char   csecPerClu;        // No. of sectors per cluster (always 16)
    short  csecReserved;      // No. of reserved sectors
    char   cFATs;             // No. of FATs (always 1)
                              // NOTE: DoubleSpace simulates 2 FATs
                              //    even though cFATs is set to 1
    short  cRootDirEntries;   // No. of root dir entries (always 512)
    short  csecTotalWORD;     // No. of total sectors
                              // NOTE: see csecTotalDWORD if 0
    char   bMedia;            // Media byte (always 0xF8 == hard disk)
    short  csecFAT;           // No. of sectors occupied by the FAT
    short  csecPerTrack;      // No. of sectors per track (ignored)
    short  cHeads;            // No. of heads (ignored)
    long   csecHidden;        // No. of hidden sectors
    long   csecTotalDWORD;    // No. of total sectors

    /*
     * The following fields are DoubleSpace extensions.
     */

    short  secMDFATStart;     // Logical sector of start of MDFAT
    char   nLog2cbPerSec;     // Log base 2 of cbPerSec
    short  csecMDReserved;    // No. of sectors before DOS BOOT sector
    short  secRootDirStart;   // First sector of root directory
    short  secHeapStart;      // First sector of sector heap
    short  cluFirstData;      // No. of MDFAT entries used for DOS boot
                              //    sector, reserved area, and root dir.
    char   cpageBitFAT;       // No. of 2K pages in the BitFAT
    short  RESERVED1;
    char   nLog2csecPerClu;   // Log base 2 of csecPerClu
    short  RESERVED2;
    long   RESERVED3;
    long   RESERVED4;
    char   f12BitFAT;         // 1 => 12-bit FAT, 0 => 16-bit FAT
    short  cmbCVFMax;         // Max CVF size, in MB (1024*1024)
} MDBPB;
```

Figure 13-2. *A C-language definition of the MDBPB structure.*

an appropriate size based on the size of the host drive. Then, it preallocates all of the other CVF structures so that they can accommodate this maximum size, even if the CVF is currently smaller than the specified maximum. That's why DoubleSpace is able to quickly increase the size of a compressed drive. Since the CVF structures are already large enough to accommodate the largest possible CVF, growing a compressed drive is as simple as resetting a few other fields in the MDBPB and allocating additional space for the CVF from the host drive.

THE BOOT PROCESS

One advantage DoubleSpace enjoys is a tight integration with MS-DOS. Earlier disk compression programs worked by loading device drivers in the CONFIG.SYS file to mount the compressed drives and swap drive letters. This arrangement led to the need to keep two copies of CONFIG.SYS: one on the uncompressed host drive, the other on the compressed C drive. This was necessary because midway through the processing of the CONFIG.SYS file, the drive letter of the boot drive changed. Without two copies of CONFIG.SYS, MS-DOS would have been lost.

DoubleSpace solves this problem by integrating disk compression into the MS-DOS kernel so that a device driver isn't required to mount the compressed drives and swap the drive letters. By the time your computer gets around to processing the CONFIG.SYS, it has already mounted the compressed drive and swapped the drive letters. Thus, only one copy of CONFIG.SYS (on the compressed drive) is required.

So that you can understand how DoubleSpace affects the way your computer boots, we'll consider the entire boot process step by step:

1. When you power on your computer, it runs a Power-On Self Test (POST) routine that quickly makes sure your computer is working properly. It is during this phase of startup that you see the copyright notice of your computer's BIOS and a count of the amount of memory you have installed.

2. When the POST is finished, the BIOS routine reads the first sector on the disk in drive A and determines whether the sector is a valid boot record. Usually, there is no disk in the drive, so the BIOS next

reads the first sector of the hard disk in the hope that it will contain a boot record. Unless something is seriously wrong, it does.

3. When the BIOS finds a valid boot record, it loads the record into memory and transfers control to it. This boot record (called the *Master Boot Record,* or *MBR*) contains a program that knows how to read the partition table, which contains a record of the partition structure on the disk. The MBR finds the active partition, reads that partition's boot record (the first sector in the partition) into memory, and transfers control to the partition's boot record.

4. The active partition's boot record contains a program that loads and runs the first MS-DOS kernel program, IO.SYS. IO.SYS, in turn, loads and runs the second MS-DOS kernel program, MSDOS.SYS.

5. Before MS-DOS 6.0, the IO.SYS file would next load and run COMMAND.COM, which would in turn process AUTO-EXEC.BAT. However, the MS-DOS 6.0 and 6.2 versions of the IO.SYS file look for a third MS-DOS kernel file: DBLSPACE.BIN. If the IO.SYS file finds DBLSPACE.BIN, it loads DBLSPACE.BIN into the top of conventional memory and transfers control to it. This begins the process of initializing DoubleSpace.

6. DBLSPACE.BIN starts out by looking for a file named DBLSPACE.INI, first on the boot drive and then on drive C (if drive C isn't the boot drive). If DBLSPACE.BIN can't find the file, it immediately unloads itself from memory and the system boots without DoubleSpace.

7. If DBLSPACE.BIN does find DBLSPACE.INI, it mounts the Compressed Volume Files specified in DBLSPACE.INI. If a CVF to be mounted is named DBLSPACE.000, DBLSPACE.BIN swaps the DBLSPACE.000 drive letter with the host's drive letter. Thus, DBLSPACE.000 on the startup volume is mounted as drive C, and a host drive letter (usually H) is assigned to the uncompressed startup volume.

8. When DBLSPACE.BIN is finished, CONFIG.SYS is processed as usual. Because DoubleSpace mounts the compressed C drive *before* CONFIG.SYS is processed, the CONFIG.SYS file is read from the compressed C drive, not from the uncompressed host.

9. If the command *Devicehigh=c:\dos\dblspace.sys /move* is present in the CONFIG.SYS file, MS-DOS runs the DBLSPACE.SYS program. This program relocates DBLSPACE.BIN from its original location at the top of conventional memory to its final location, either in an Upper Memory Block (if one is available) or at the bottom of conventional memory, where it won't interfere with application programs.

   DBLSPACE.SYS confuses many people. It's required because memory management isn't integrated as tightly with MS-DOS as DoubleSpace is. You want to load the 43KB DBLSPACE.BIN program (or even MS-DOS 6.2's 34KB or 38KB DBLSPACE.BIN) into upper memory if possible. However, upper memory doesn't exist until it has been created by the EMM386.EXE program. And EMM386.EXE is loaded when MS-DOS processes CONFIG.SYS, long after DBLSPACE.BIN has been loaded into memory. MS-DOS obviously can't initially locate DBLSPACE.BIN in upper memory. Hence the DBLSPACE.SYS program: its only purpose in life is to move DBLSPACE.BIN to its final location, either in upper memory or at the bottom of conventional memory. Once DBLSPACE.BIN has been relocated, DBLSPACE.SYS removes itself from memory.

10. If CONFIG.SYS doesn't contain a Devicehigh command to load DBLSPACE.SYS or if you load DBLSPACE.SYS with a Device command instead of a Devicehigh command, DBLSPACE.BIN is automatically relocated near the bottom of conventional memory.

THE DBLSPACE.INI FILE

DBLSPACE.INI is a text file that controls how DoubleSpace starts. It lives on your boot drive, which is either your uncompressed C drive or the host drive for your compressed C drive (usually H).

MS-DOS 6.2 provides Dblspace command-line switches that let you change the settings in DBLSPACE.INI without editing the file. These switches are described in detail in the appendix.

If you're using MS-DOS 6.0, you must edit DBLSPACE.INI to change its settings. DBLSPACE.INI is marked as a system, hidden, read-only file, so you have to change its attributes before you can edit it. Use this command to change the attributes:

```
H:\> attrib dblspace.ini -s -h -r
```

When you've finished editing DBLSPACE.INI, reset the attributes with this command:

```
H:\> attrib dblspace.ini +s +h +r
```

Warning: Don't mess around with this file if you're not sure of what you're doing. Mess up this file, and you might not be able to access your compressed drives. That would be bad.

A typical DBLSPACE.INI file looks something like this:

```
MaxRemovableDrives=2
FirstDrive=D
LastDrive=H
MaxFileFragments=123
ActivateDrive=H,C0
```

MaxRemovableDrives

The *MaxRemovableDrives* line is a little misleading. It specifies how many additional compressed drives you can mount after your system has started. Usually, you should set *MaxRemovableDrives* to the number of floppy drives you have. However, you should also allow for a removable hard drive if you have one. And if you plan on mounting a compressed RAM drive, you should allow for it too.

FirstDrive

The *FirstDrive* line indicates the drive letter of the first drive that's available for DoubleSpace to use. Usually, this is one drive letter higher than the highest real drive on the system. For example, if you have just a C drive, *FirstDrive* is set to *D*. If you have a C and a D drive, *FirstDrive* is set to *E*.

DoubleSpace itself sets *FirstDrive,* so you shouldn't mess with it. If you set *FirstDrive* to a drive letter that's used by a real drive (drive C, for instance), your computer might go haywire, possibly rebooting itself over and over again.

LastDrive

The *LastDrive* line indicates the last drive letter that's available for DoubleSpace to use. Normally, DoubleSpace sets *LastDrive* to four letters higher than *FirstDrive*. So if *FirstDrive* is *D*, *LastDrive* will be *H*.

When DoubleSpace assigns drive letters, it starts at *LastDrive* and works backwards towards *FirstDrive*. That's why the host for drive C is assigned drive letter H, and if you later create a new compressed drive on the same host, it's assigned drive letter G.

If you change the *LastDrive* setting, make sure you don't specify a drive letter that's more than 13 drive letters past *FirstDrive*. And don't set *LastDrive* so high that there aren't any drive letters left for drives created by device drivers loaded in CONFIG.SYS, such as CD-ROM drives or RAM drives.

MaxFileFragments

The *MaxFileFragments* line specifies the maximum amount of fragmentation that's permissible for your CVFs. This field is a little confusing, so bear with me. I'm not talking about fragmentation of compressed files stored in the CVF; instead, I'm talking about fragmentation of the CVF itself. In other words, if the host drive doesn't have enough contiguous disk space to hold the entire CVF, the CVF is fragmented.

During installation, DoubleSpace sets *MaxFileFragments* to *2600*. Such a high number is called for because compressing your C drive in place often results in a highly fragmented CVF, especially if you didn't run Defrag before installing DoubleSpace. Thereafter, every time you mount a CVF, the *MaxFileFragments* value is set to the actual number of file fragments in all CVFs, plus 110. The extra 110 fragments are provided to let you grow the CVF.

ActivateDrive

DBLSPACE.INI contains one *ActivateDrive* line for each compressed volume to be mounted. It's roughly equivalent to the Dblspace /mount command. Although you can include as many *ActivateDrive* lines in DBLSPACE.INI as you want, only the first 15 are processed. That means that if you have more than 15 compressed drives, you have to mount drives 16, 17, 18, and so on by putting Dblspace /mount commands in your AUTOEXEC.BAT file.

The *ActivateDrive* line in DBLSPACE.INI is a little confusing. To make sure you fully understand it, let's take a look at its Official Syntax:

```
ActivateDrive=X,Yn
```

X has a different meaning depending on the value of Yn, so we'll start with Yn: it indicates which CVF is to be mounted. Y represents the physical drive that contains the CVF, *before* any other drive letter changes have been made. In other words, if the CVF resides on your first hard drive, Y should be C because the first hard drive is always drive C.

The number you type for n corresponds to the CVF's extension. Thus, $C0$ represents the file DBLSPACE.000 on physical drive C, $C1$ represents DBLSPACE.001, and so on.

If n is 0, X represents the drive letter you want to be assigned to the host drive. DoubleSpace plays a little shell game with the drive letters for the CVF named DBLSPACE.000. First, it mounts the CVF as drive X. Then, it quickly swaps the host and CVF drive letters. The result of this exchange is that the host drive is accessed as drive X and the CVF is mounted as drive Y.

So (watch carefully) this command,

```
ActivateDrive=H,C0
```

says to mount the CVF DBLSPACE.000 on drive C as drive H and then to swap the drive letters so that the compressed drive is accessed as drive C and the host drive is accessed as drive H.

If n is greater than 0, X represents the drive letter you want the compressed drive mounted as. So this command,

```
ActivateDrive=D,C1
```

says to mount the CVF DBLSPACE.001 on physical drive C as drive D. Notice here that even though a previous *ActivateDrive* line has swapped the host drive letter, you still specify the host's physical drive letter.

AutoMount (MS-DOS 6.2 Only)

The *AutoMount* line controls the MS-DOS 6.2 Automount feature. To enable this feature, the following line should appear in DBLSPACE.INI:

```
AutoMount=1
```

To disable the feature, this line is used:

```
AutoMount=0
```

To enable Automount for a specific drive (in this case, drive A):

```
AutoMount=A
```

And to enable Automount for several drives, a line like this one is used:

```
AutoMount=AD
```

In this example, Automount is activated for drives A and D.

DoubleGuard (MS-DOS 6.2 Only)

The *DoubleGuard* line controls the DoubleGuard feature of MS-DOS 6.2. To activate DoubleGuard, this line is added to DBLSPACE.INI:

```
DoubleGuard=1
```

To disable DoubleGuard, this line should appear in DBLSPACE.INI:

```
DoubleGuard=0
```

ROMServer (MS-DOS 6.2 Only)

The *ROMServer* line controls whether or not DoubleSpace should look for a hardware-based MRCI server. If this line is included in DBLSPACE.INI,

```
ROMServer=1
```

DoubleSpace checks to see if a hardware-based MRCI server is present. This line:

```
ROMServer=0
```

disables the check. *ROMServer=1* should be specified only if you're certain that your computer has a hardware-based MRCI server.

Switches (MS-DOS 6.2 Only)

The *Switches* line controls the ability to disable DoubleSpace by pressing Ctrl+F5 or Ctrl+F8 when you boot your computer. If *Switches* is not present in DBLSPACE.INI, you can use Ctrl+F5 or Ctrl+F8 to disable DoubleSpace. If this line is in DBLSPACE.INI:

```
Switches=/F
```

the Ctrl+F5 and Ctrl+F8 are ignored, so you can't bypass DoubleSpace when you start your computer. This line:

```
Switches=/N
```

reduces the amount of time MS-DOS waits for you to press Ctrl+F5 or Ctrl+F8. This can make your computer start faster, but you have to press Ctrl+F5 or Ctrl+F8 quicker if you want to disable DoubleSpace.

/F and /N can be used together:

```
Switches=/F/N
```

This command ignores the Ctrl+F5 and Ctrl+F8 keys altogether and speeds up your system startup.

THE DOUBLESPACE API

If you're a programmer, you might want to know about one more aspect of how DoubleSpace works: the DoubleSpace System Application Programming Interface (API). The functions available through the DoubleSpace API are provided by DBLSPACE.BIN, so they're not available if DBLSPACE.BIN isn't loaded.

Since DoubleSpace simulates a standard MS-DOS drive, most application programs don't need to use any of the specialized DoubleSpace functions this API provides. Special-purpose utility programs do, however. If you're wondering how utility programs such as *Norton Disk Doctor* work or if you're thinking of writing a DoubleSpace utility program of your own, you'll be interested to see what functions are provided by the DoubleSpace API.

I'm not going to describe each function call in detail here. Instead, I'll just give you an overview of what each function does. If you want to, you can study the program in the sidebar "ISDS: A Simple DoubleSpace Utility." For more information, consult the *MS-DOS Programmer's Reference 6.0*.

Function	Description
DSFlushCache	Flushes (writes to disk) all of Double-Space's internal caches.
DSFlushAndInvalidateCache	Works as DSFlushCache does but also invalidates the caches. Used by defragmenters, disk repair programs, and other utilities.
DSGetVersion	Returns the DoubleSpace version number, the letter of the first drive reserved for use by DoubleSpace, and the number of drives reserved.

ISDS: A Simple DoubleSpace Utility

The *DSGetDriveMapping* function can be used to create a simple utility program that indicates whether or not a particular drive is compressed. This utility, named *ISDS*, sets the MS-DOS *Errorlevel* to *1* if the current drive is compressed; if the current drive is not compressed, ISDS sets *Errorlevel* to *0*. You can use ISDS in a batch file by first making the drive you want to test the current drive, running ISDS, and then testing *Errorlevel* with an If command.

To create the ISDS utility, create the following text file using the MS-DOS Edit command:

```
a    100
mov  ah,19    ; Int 21 Function 19
int  21       ; Get Default Drive (A=0, B=1, etc.)
mov  dl,al    ; dl=drive letter
mov  ax,4a11  ; required for DSGetDriveMapping function
mov  bx,1     ; DSGetDriveMapping function
int  2f       ; Int 2f is DoubleSpace multiplex
or   ax,ax    ; ax!=0 means failure
jnz  11b      ; exit if failure
test bl,80    ; bl AND 80 true if compressed drive
jz   11b      ; exit if not compressed
mov  al,1     ; set Errorlevel to 1
jmp  11d      ; jump to exit
mov  al,0     ; (11b) Set Errorlevel to 0
```

DSGetDriveMapping	Indicates whether a particular drive is compressed and, if it is, indicates the drive's host drive.
DSSwapDrive	Swaps the drive letter of a compressed drive with the letter of its host drive. Intended for use only by DBLSPACE.EXE.
DSGetEntryPoints	Returns the entry points for a Double-Space drive's routines.
DSSetEntryPoints	Sets the entry points for a DoubleSpace drive's routines.
DSActivateDrive	Mounts a compressed drive.
DSDeactivateDrive	Unmounts a compressed drive.
DSGetDriveSpace	Returns the total number of sectors and the number of free sectors in a compressed drive's sector heap.

(continued)

```
mov  ah,4c    ; (11d) Int 21 Function 4c
int  21       ; exit program

r cx
22
n isds.com
w
q
```

Be sure to create the file exactly as shown, including the blank line just before the *r cx* line. Name the file ISDS.SCR.

Next, use the MS-DOS Debug command as follows to create the ISDS.COM file:

```
C:\> debug <isds.scr
```

Here's a batch file named TESTDS.BAT that uses ISDS:

```
@echo off
isds
if Errorlevel 1 goto isds
echo Current drive is not compressed
goto Exit
:isds
echo Current drive is compressed
:Exit
```

continued

Function	Description
DSGetFileFragmentSpace	Returns the DBLSPACE.INI *MaxFileFragments* setting.
DSGetExtraInfo ·	Returns the number of drives allocated for DoubleSpace. This number equals the number of drives successfully mounted by the DBLSPACE.INI *ActivateDrive* lines plus the number of removable drives reserved by *MaxRemovableDrives*. ·

All of these functions except *DSFlushCache* and *DSFlushAndInvalidate-Cache* are called via the MS-DOS multiplex interrupt, Int 2Fh. The DoubleSpace functions are assigned multiplex number 4A11h. The two cache functions are called via the IOCTL function, Int 21h Function 4404h.

■ Remember that the functions for actually compressing and decompressing data are provided by MRCI, not by the DoubleSpace API.

■ You might have noticed that DoubleSpace does not provide functions for accessing data in the MDFAT or other CVF structures. For example, there's no function that returns the starting sector number for a particular cluster. Programs that need that kind of information have to get it the hard way: by manually scanning the directory, FAT, and MDFAT entries. The information a program needs to navigate these structures is found in the MDBPB, which is always the first sector in a CVF.

CONCLUSION

The information in this chapter is more than you need to know to use DoubleSpace. If you're curious about how DoubleSpace works or about how utility programs like *Norton Disk Doctor* can check the internal structure of a CVF, I hope this chapter has satiated your curiosity. If it hasn't, you'll find more information about DoubleSpace and the CVF structure in the *Microsoft MS-DOS Programmer's Reference*.

SUMMARY

- MRCI is a data compression standard developed by Microsoft for DoubleSpace and Microsoft Backup. Presumably, we'll soon see MRCI compatible hardware that significantly boosts the performance of DoubleSpace.

- The root directory and the FAT of a compressed drive are the same as for an uncompressed drive.

- The MDFAT is an extended FAT that lets DoubleSpace keep track of the CVF sectors assigned to each cluster.

- The sector heap is the area of the CVF from which sectors are allocated to file clusters.

- The BitFAT keeps track of which sectors in the sector heap are used and which are free.

- The MDBPB is an important structure that contains information about the configuration of a DoubleSpace drive.

- DBLSPACE.BIN is loaded when your computer boots. It automatically mounts as many as 15 compressed drives specified by the DBLSPACE.INI file.

- DBLSPACE.SYS is required in the CONFIG.SYS file if you want to relocate DBLSPACE.BIN to upper memory.

- The DBLSPACE.INI file contains a variety of settings that control how DoubleSpace starts. Change these settings only if you know what you're doing!

- For programmers, DoubleSpace provides an API that allows manipulation of compressed drives.

Etcetera, etcetera, etcetera.

—The King and I

Appendix

Dblspace
Command Summary

This appendix is a complete summary of the MS-DOS Dblspace command switches. Keep it handy for reference.

Note: All Dblspace command switches can be abbreviated to shorter forms, as long as you type at least enough characters to uniquely identify the switch to Dblspace. For example, you can abbreviate /defragment as /defrag or /def but not as /de because Dblspace wouldn't know whether /de meant /defragment or /delete.

DBLSPACE

If you use the Dblspace command by itself with no switches, you start up the Dblspace program. Then, you can select DoubleSpace functions by means of easy-to-use menus and dialog boxes.

Notes

- You can't run Dblspace while *Windows* is running or while the MS-DOS shell's task switcher is active. (In MS-DOS 6.2, you can run the Dblspace /info and /list commands while *Windows* is running.)

- The first time you run Dblspace, you start up the DoubleSpace installation routine.

- The Dblspace command has a variety of switches that call various functions. All of the switches are described in this appendix.

DBLSPACE /AUTOMOUNT (MS-DOS 6.2 ONLY)

The Dblspace /automount command enables or disables the Automount feature for MS-DOS 6.2.

```
dblspace /automount=0¦1¦A...Z
```

The /automount switch controls the Automount feature. Specify *0* to disable Automount, *1* to enable it, or one or more drive letters to enable Automount just for specific drives.

Notes

- The default setting for the Automount feature is for the automatic mounting of all drives.

- The /automount switch changes the *AutoMount* setting in the DBLSPACE.INI file. You must restart your computer for the change to take effect.

DBLSPACE /CHKDSK (MS-DOS 6.0 ONLY)

The Dblspace /chkdsk command checks the integrity of the internal structure of a compressed drive. It is analogous to the MS-DOS Chkdsk command, which checks a drive's FAT structure.

```
dblspace /chkdsk [/f]
```

If you use the /f switch, Dblspace not only checks the compressed drive for errors but also corrects any errors it finds.

Notes

- The Chkdsk command has been made obsolete in MS-DOS 6.2. Use the ScanDisk command instead.

- When you use the Chkdsk command to check the structure of a compressed drive in MS-DOS 6.0, Chkdsk automatically runs the Dblspace /chkdsk command, so there's usually no need to run Dblspace /chkdsk separately.

DBLSPACE /COMPRESS

The Dblspace /compress command creates a compressed drive by compressing the data on an uncompressed drive. Note that the Dblspace /create command (below) creates a new, empty compressed drive.

```
dblspace /compress drive1:
        [/newdrive=drive2:] [/reserve=size] [/f]
```

drive1: identifies the uncompressed drive to be compressed.

/newdrive=*drive2:* specifies the drive letter to use for the host drive. If you omit this switch, Dblspace picks the drive letter.

/reserve=*size* specifies how many megabytes of disk space to leave free on the host drive. The default is *2*.

/f prevents Dblspace from displaying the final screen when compression is complete (MS-DOS 6.2 only).

Notes

- To compress your C drive, you must have at least 1.2MB of free disk space on it. To compress any other hard drive, you must have at least 1.1MB of free disk space on it. To compress a floppy disk, you must have 0.5MB of free space on it.

- DoubleSpace can't compress a 360KB floppy disk.

- The Dblspace /compress command automatically mounts the compressed drive it creates. However, you must manually mount a compressed floppy if you remove it from the drive and access another disk in that drive or restart your computer—unless you use the MS-DOS 6.2 Automount feature.

DBLSPACE /CREATE

The Dblspace /create command creates an empty compressed drive out of free space on an existing uncompressed drive. Note that the Dblspace /compress command (above) creates a compressed drive by compressing the data on an existing uncompressed drive.

```
dblspace /create drive1:
        [/newdrive=drive2:] [/size=size|/reserve=size]
```

drive1: identifies the uncompressed drive on which the compressed drive is to be created.

/newdrive=*drive2:* specifies the drive letter to use for the new empty compressed drive. If you omit this switch, Dblspace picks the drive letter.

/size=*size* specifies how many megabytes of disk space to use for the new empty compressed drive. The default is *2*.

/reserve=*size* specifies how many megabytes of disk space to leave free on the host drive. You can specify /size or /reserve, but not both. If you omit both, DoubleSpace reserves 2MB on the host.

Notes

- The Dblspace /create command automatically mounts the compressed drive.

- To make the compressed drive as large as possible, specify */reserve=0*.

DBLSPACE /DEFRAGMENT

The Dblspace /defragment command defragments the internal structure of a compressed drive so that available free space is consolidated.

```
dblspace /defragment [drive:] [/f]
```

drive: specifies the compressed drive you want to defragment. If you omit it, Dblspace defragments the current drive.

/f defragments the drive more completely than the default defragmenting process.

Notes

- The MS-DOS Defrag command defragments both compressed and noncompressed drives. After MS-DOS Defrag defragments a compressed drive, it runs the Dblspace /defragment command to defragment the internal structure of the compressed drive.

- To defragment a drive as much as possible, run these two commands in a batch file:

```
dblspace /defrag /f
defrag
```

- If you are unable to reduce the size of a compressed drive, you might need to defragment it first.

DBLSPACE /DELETE

Dblspace /delete is a dangerous command: it deletes an entire compressed drive. Don't use this command unless you know what you're doing.

```
dblspace /delete drive:
```

drive: specifies the compressed drive you want to delete.

Notes

- You can't delete drive C.

- Dangerous command! Don't play with it!

DBLSPACE /DOUBLEGUARD (MS-DOS 6.2 ONLY)

The Dblspace /doubleguard command activates or deactivates the DoubleGuard feature of MS-DOS 6.2.

```
dblspace /doubleguard=[0¦1]
```

Specify *0* to disable DoubleGuard or *1* to enable it.

Notes

- DoubleGuard is enabled by default.

- The /doubleguard switch changes the *DoubleGuard* setting in DBLSPACE.INI. You must restart your computer for the change to take effect.

DBLSPACE /FORMAT

The Dblspace /format command formats a compressed drive. This completely erases the data on the drive, so be sure you know what you're doing before you use it.

```
dblspace /format drive:
```

drive: specifies the compressed drive you want to format.

Notes

- You can't format drive C.

- You can't use the MS-DOS Format command to format a compressed drive. Format is one of the few MS-DOS commands that doesn't automatically run its Dblspace counterpart on a compressed drive.

- Dangerous command! Don't play with it!

DBLSPACE /HOST

The Dblspace /host command changes the drive letter assigned to a host drive.

```
dblspace drive1: /host=drive2:
```

drive 1: specifies the compressed drive whose host drive letter you want to change. Alternatively, you can specify the host drive letter here.

drive 2: specifies the new drive letter you want to be assigned to the host drive.

Notes

- The /host switch changes the host drive letter used in the *ActivateDrive* line in DBLSPACE.INI. You must restart your computer for the change to take effect.

DBLSPACE /INFO

The Dblspace /info command displays various items of information about a compressed drive.

```
dblspace [/info] drive:
```

drive: specifies the drive whose information you want to be displayed.

Notes

- /info can be omitted if you specify the drive letter.

- The information displayed includes the name of the Compressed Volume File, the space used, the actual compression ratio achieved for files on the drive, the drive's free space, the estimated compression ratio used to calculate the free space, the percentage of the drive that is fragmented, and the total space taken up by the CVF.

DBLSPACE /LASTDRIVE (MS-DOS 6.2 ONLY)

The Dblspace /lastdrive command sets the highest drive letter (the letter latest in the alphabet) that's reserved for DoubleSpace's use.

```
dblspace /lastdrive=drive
```

drive is the highest drive letter that can be used by DoubleSpace.

Notes

- The /lastdrive switch changes the *LastDrive* setting in the DBLSPACE.INI file. You must restart your computer for the change to take effect.

- Don't set *LastDrive* to a letter that is lower (that is, earlier in the alphabet) than any drive letter currently used by DoubleSpace.

DBLSPACE /LIST

The Dblspace /list command lists all of your computer's drives (except network drives) with a brief description of each drive.

```
dblspace /list
```

DBLSPACE /MAXFILEFRAGMENTS (MS-DOS 6.2 ONLY)

The Dblspace /maxfilefragments command sets the maximum allowable fragmentation level for DoubleSpace CVFs.

```
dblspace /maxfilefragments=n
```

n is the maximum number of CVF file fragments allowed for all mounted compressed drives.

Notes

■ The /maxfilefragments switch changes the *MaxFileFragments* setting in DBLSPACE.INI. You must restart your computer for the change to take effect.

DBLSPACE /MAXREMOVABLEDRIVES (MS-DOS 6.2 ONLY)

The Dblspace /maxremovabledrives command sets the number of additional compressed drives you can mount beyond those that are mounted automatically at startup.

```
dblspace /maxremovabledrives=n
```

n specifies how many compressed drives can be mounted in addition to those that are mounted when you start up your system.

Notes

■ The /maxremovabledrives switch changes the *MaxRemovableDrives* setting in DBLSPACE.INI. You must restart your computer for the change to take effect.

DBLSPACE /MOUNT

The Dblspace /mount command mounts a compressed drive.

```
dblspace /mount[=nnn] drive1: [/newdrive=drive2:]
```

nnn specifies the extension of the Compressed Volume File you want to mount; for example, to mount DBLSPACE.001, you would specify */mount=001*. If you omit *nnn*, Dblspace mounts DBLSPACE.000.

drive1: specifies the uncompressed drive that contains the CVF you want to mount.

/newdrive=drive2: specifies the drive letter you want to be assigned to the compressed drive. If you omit this switch, DoubleSpace picks the drive.

Notes

■ DoubleSpace normally mounts compressed hard drives automatically, so you'll probably use the /mount switch only for floppy drives or removable hard drives.

DBLSPACE /RATIO

The Dblspace /ratio command sets the compression ratio used to calculate free space remaining on a compressed drive.

```
dblspace /ratio[=ratio] [drive:¦/all]
```

ratio specifies the ratio you want Dblspace to use to estimate free space. *ratio* can include one decimal place—for example, *1.7, 2.0, 2.5*. If you omit *ratio*, DoubleSpace uses the average compression ratio achieved for the files already on the drive.

drive: specifies the drive whose ratio you want to change.

all specifies that the ratio for all compressed drives should be changed. If you omit *drive:* and *all*, DoubleSpace sets the ratio for the current drive.

Notes

■ DoubleSpace does *not* automatically set the compression ratio for all drives to the actual ratio every time you restart your computer. If you want DoubleSpace to do that, add the command *Dblspace /ratio /all* to your AUTOEXEC.BAT file.

DBLSPACE /ROMSERVER (MS-DOS 6.2 ONLY)

The Dblspace /romserver command tells DoubleSpace whether or not it should search for a hardware-based MRCI server.

```
dblspace /romserver=[0¦1]
```

To enable the search for a hardware-based MRCI server, specify */romserver=1*; to disable the search, specify */romserver=0*.

Notes

■ The hardware-based MRCI server search is disabled by default.

■ The /romserver switch changes the *ROMServer* setting in DBLSPACE.INI. You must restart your computer for the change to take effect.

DBLSPACE /SIZE

The Dblspace /size command changes the size of a compressed drive.

```
dblspace /size[=size1 ¦ /reserve=size2] drive:
```

size1 specifies the new size of the compressed drive in megabytes.

size2 specifies the amount of free space to leave on the host. DoubleSpace adjusts the size of the compressed drive accordingly.

If you omit *size1* and *size2*, DoubleSpace makes the compressed drive as small as possible.

drive: specifies the drive you want to resize.

Notes

■ There are three ways to specify the new size for the compressed drive. First, you can specify the size in the /size switch:

```
dblspace /size=100
```

This specification sets the size of the compressed drive to 100MB. Second, you can specify the host size in the /reserve switch:

```
dblspace /size /reserve=10
```

This specification leaves 10MB of free space on the host drive. Third, you can omit both *size1* and *size2*; DoubleSpace will make the compressed drive as small as possible.

■ If DoubleSpace is unable to change the size of the drive, you might need to run Dblspace /defrag or the MS-DOS Defrag command to defragment the drive.

DBLSPACE /SWITCHES (MS-DOS 6.2 ONLY)

The Dblspace /switches command controls the clean boot feature of MS-DOS 6.2.

```
dblspace /switches=[n¦f¦nf]
```

Specify */switches=n* to disable clean booting (that is, booting without DoubleSpace—Ctrl+F5 or Ctrl+F8). Specify */switches=f* to reduce the amount of time MS-DOS waits for the user to press Ctrl+F5 or Ctrl+F8. Specify */switches=nf* to disable clean booting and reduce the wait time.

Notes

- The clean boot feature is enabled by default.

- The /switches switch changes the *Switches* setting in the DBLSPACE.INI file. You must restart your computer for the change to take effect.

- In MS-DOS 6.2, you must manually edit DBLSPACE.INI to remove the *Switches* setting.

DBLSPACE /UNCOMPRESS (MS-DOS 6.2 ONLY)

The Dblspace /uncompress command uncompresses a compressed DoubleSpace drive.

```
dblspace /uncompress [drive:]
```

drive: is the compressed drive to be uncompressed.

Notes

- DoubleSpace uncompresses a drive by moving its compressed data to the compressed drive's host drive and then deleting the compressed drive's CVF.

- You can't uncompress a drive if it contains more data than will fit on the host drive in uncompressed form.

- When you uncompress the last DoubleSpace drive on your system, Dblspace asks if you want to remove the DoubleSpace system files from the root directory of your boot drive. This effectively uninstalls DoubleSpace.

DBLSPACE /UNMOUNT

The Dblspace /unmount command unmounts a compressed drive. This makes the drive temporarily inaccessible.

```
dblspace /unmount [drive:]
```

drive: specifies the drive you want to unmount. If you omit *drive:*, the current drive is unmounted.

Notes

- You can't unmount drive C.

DBLSPACE.SYS

A reference to the DBLSPACE.SYS file is used in the CONFIG.SYS file to relocate the DBLSPACE.BIN file to its final location in memory.

```
Device=c:\dos\dblspace.sys /move [/nohma]
```

```
Devicehigh=c:\dos\dblspace.sys /move [/nohma]
```

/move is required. It identifies the function of DBLSPACE.SYS, which is relocating the DBLSPACE.BIN file to its final memory location.

The optional */nohma* prevents DBLSPACE.SYS from moving a part of DBLSPACE.BIN into the high memory area (MS-DOS 6.2 only).

Notes

- If DBLSPACE.SYS is loaded with a Device command, the DBLSPACE.BIN file is relocated to the bottom of conventional memory.

- If DBLSPACE.SYS is loaded with a Devicehigh command, the DBLSPACE.BIN file is relocated to upper memory if possible.

- A Device command to load DBLSPACE.SYS is automatically added to your CONFIG.SYS file when you install DoubleSpace. If you have a 386 or 486 computer, you should edit CONFIG.SYS and change the Device command to a Devicehigh command.

Index

Note: *Italic* page-number references indicate figures and tables.

Special Characters

386SPART.PAR permanent swap file for *Windows*, 22, 23, 28, 127–28, 132–34

A

active partition, 173
/ah switch (Dir command), 23
allocation units. *See* clusters (allocation units)
ALLSTACK command, 149
/all switch, 79, 192
Application Programming Interface (API), DoubleSpace, 179–82
application programs, 118
arms on disks, 9–10
ASCII, 12
ASCII text (.TXT) file compression ratio, 2
/as switch (Dir command), 123
ATTRIB.EXE file, panic disk copy, 43
AUTOEXEC.BAT file
  bypassing, 108
  Chkdsk command, 46
  Dblspace /mount command, 106
  Dblspace /ratio /all command, 192
  Dir command to display compression ratios, 60
  Image command, 111
  memory resident program commands, 108
  Mirror command, 111
  MOUSE command, 71
  panic disk copy, 43
  RAM drive compression commands, 93
  selectively processing lines in, 108
  SMARTDrive command, 66–68
  Stacker drive conversion and, 147

AUTOEXEC.BAT file, *continued*
  temporary command added, 36
automatic mounting of drives, 104–6, 185
Automount feature xiii, 98, 102, 104–106, 185
/automount switch (MS-DOS 6.2 only), 104–5, 185

B

Backup command, 60. *See also* Microsoft Backup (Msbackup)
backup (.BAK) files, 140
backup programs, floppy disk copy, 43
backups. *See also* Microsoft Backup (Msbackup)
  differential, 61, 62
  incremental, 61, 62
  system, 28–29
.BAK (backup) files, 140
base-2 (binary) numbers, 10–12
base-10 (decimal) numbers, 11
batch (.BAT) file compression ratio, 2
batch file to compress floppies, 101
.BAT (batch) file compression ratio, 2
binary digits (bits), 11–12
binary files, 155
binary (base-2) numbers, 10–12
BIOS Parameter Block (BPB), 170
BitFAT. *See* Bit-mapped File Allocation Table
bitmap (.MBP) file compression ratio, 2
Bit-mapped File Allocation Table (BitFAT), 170
bits (binary digits), 11–12
.BMP (bitmap) file compression ratio, 2
booting clean, 108, 193–94
boot process, 172–74
boot record, 172–73

DOUG LOWE

Doug Lowe has been involved in computer book publishing since 1977. He has written 15 books on various computer subjects, which have together sold more than 500,000 copies. He got his start writing esoteric tomes on subjects of interest only to professionals who worked with mainframe computers (remember mainframe computers?), but his more recent books have had a broader appeal.

Doug is a DoubleSpace fanatic who is convinced that too few people have experienced the benefits of what he calls "this amazing but totally confusing program." He is considered by many Microsoft insiders to be personally responsible for most of the 5 million copies of the MS-DOS 6.0 upgrade that have been sold so far. (Not!)

Doug lives in sunny Fresno, California (where the motto is *We're Close to San Francisco*), with his wife, Debbie, their daughters Rebecca, Sarah, and Bethany, and Nutmeg and Ginger, two golden retriever puppies who love to shred unedited manuscripts.

The manuscript for this book was prepared and submitted to Microsoft Press in electronic form. Text files were prepared using Microsoft Word 2.0 for Windows. Pages were composed by Microsoft Press using PageMaker 4.2 for Windows, with text in Times Roman and display type in Helvetica Bold. Composed pages were delivered to the printer as electronic prepress files.

Cover Designer
Rebecca Geisler

Cover Color Separator
Color Service, Inc.

Interior Graphic Designer
Kim Eggleston

Interior Graphic Artist
Lisa Sandburg

Principal Typographer
Carolyn M. Davids

Principal Editorial Compositor
John Sugg

Principal Proofreader/Copy Editor
Deborah Long

Indexer
Foxon-Maddocks Associates

Printed on recycled paper stock.